NEW EARTH –
NEW TRUTH

A God-Mind Plan for Saving Planet and Man

as revealed to
Jean K. Foster

Uni★Sun
Kansas City

Request for such permission should be addressed to:

Uni*Sun
P.O. Box 25421
Kansas City, MO 64119

This book is manufactured in the United States of
America. Cover art by Daniel, Richter & Rood
Distribution by The Talman Company:

The Talman Company, Inc.
150 Fifth Avenue
New York, NY 10011

Library of Congress Cataloging-in-Publication Data

Foster, Jean K.
  New earth--new truth: a God-mind plan for saving planet
and man/
Jean K. Foster
      p.   cm. -- (The textbook trilogy; 1)
    ISBN 0-912949-29-5 $9.95
    1. New Age movement. 2. Spirit writings I. Title II. Series
BP605.N48F67   1989
299' .93--dc 19   CIP 88-51918

A
Uni*Sun
BOOK

Thank You for Your Help

Evelyn Harris

Gail Tucker

and editor/partner Carl B. Foster

Table of Contents

CONTENTS

Earth-mind truth has taken over planet earth which is rapidly deteriorating. Therefore, it is time to turn to the supreme truth which will bring you and planet earth into perfection, into purity and into oneness with what is God.

Advanced spirits work to help those in the earth plane in their present lifetime experiences and to prepare them for living in the New Age.

Now is the time to accept the offer of the tender presences who will help you visualize and use your God-mind truth in a practical, generous way.

God-mind truth must be used if it is going to help us grow spiritually and manifest whatever is needed.

Nothing in your life changes unless you learn how to center your being and make your God-mind connection. A message from Jesus brings this point home.

Only those who accept God-mind truth and reject earth-mind truth will survive successfully in the New Age.

The Brotherhood explains the principles of eternal truth which will help anyone meet the needs of the New Age.

CONTENTS

CONTENTS

Dedication

"New Earth—New Truth" is dedicated to the following spirit entity and to all other spirit entities from the next plane of life who are now working to put new truth into planet earth.*

This witness identified himself as an ornithologist, writer and lecturer in his past lifetime. His message began:

The birds have been among the first to know of earth's problems. They who fly freely in the open sky sing their songs to those who have ears to hear.

"Never the same," they lament. "Not the way it was," they mourn. "Where are the abundant supplies? What has happened to our Giver of Gifts?"

The birds cry out, and I now hear and understand their songs. You who enter into the truth proclaimed here will be the ones to give these precious birds the answers they seek. And when you give them their answers, you will be giving the answers to earth itself, to those who live upon the earth and to those who will live upon the earth again.

---

*In the section called "Witnesses," concerned spirit entities speak out about the needs of earth and what we (those in the next plane and we in the earth plane) can do to help.

Preface
by Jean K. Foster

There is no time left for petty thoughts and frivolous attitudes. The time of the New Age is upon us, readers.
The day is approaching with eternal certainty when your
truth will stand or fall in its practical worth. Why wait to
see what happens next? Why be the one who resists
change? Become the God truth in expression, for then you
will know true gentleness, true prosperity and true methods by which you can bring the good of life into form.

*The advanced spirits of the Brotherhood of God, those who
live in the next plane of life in order to help us to make our
God-mind connections, thus set the tone of the first book of
the second trilogy that comes through me but certainly not
from me.*

*The first trilogy of books—the Trilogy of Truth, explains
how to make an individual God-mind connection, how to
claim both the personal and eternal God truth and finally, how
to use truth in effecting changes in ourselves and in the world
about us and how to manifest whatever we need or desire.*

*This second trilogy is directed entirely toward the New Age,
that period of the earth's redevelopment that will result in
upheaval and a great "stirring up." However, the message of
this book, as well as the next two, is not one of disaster, nor is
it a description of cataclysmic events. It is one of hope for
those spirits in human form who want to participate creatively
with the great renewal of planet earth.*

Team Up!— The Clarion Cry

1

Can I have a partnership with God that will solve problems, meet every emergency, calm my fears and confidently take me into the New Age?

Now is the time to put your truth to work, *the messenger from the Brotherhood of God began.* We in the next plane of life who now enter the earth plane to give this message, team up with this writer to put the whole teamwork of God into perspective. To understand the perspective, however, it is necessary for you to know that the reality of earth's people is spirit, not their body selves.

The truth of God, that which is incorruptible, eternal and perfect, is ready for your use. The teamwork that you want and need emanates through the God of the Universe into your own being and is helped along by those who call themselves the Brotherhood of God. This teamwork undoubtedly will combine the Pure Truth with your being. And once the truth is within you, the advanced ones will show you how to make it work in your earth experience.

The New Age is upon us, according to the advanced spirits who are the Brotherhood of God. They want this book to awaken people to the necessity of putting God truth to work in

*their lives. They say earth-mind truth urges people to put off
what seems inevitable and fearsome.*

The way of earth truth lies in the path of getting no-
where, *they insist.*

*Therefore, they bring this new book to readers who awaken
their minds so they will know how to proceed. It is not
enough, the message says, merely to accept the truth they
bring.* To make truth work in your lifetime experience is
the object! *they announce vigorously.* What good is truth,
they ask, if it does not help you to overcome difficult experiences? What good is truth if there is nothing demonstrated in the outer earth life?

*Those who bring these words explain that they are ad-
vanced spirits who stay nearby in the next plane of life to give
us counsel and to help us tap into a flow of wisdom called God-
mind. They are "the more visible proof of God" whose assignment is to help us in the earth plane to live our lives to the fullest. In the* Trilogy of Truth*, *the role of the Brotherhood was
discussed in detail. And now, in this second trilogy, the message of the Brotherhood is even more direct.*

The Pure Truth is what we want to discuss first. To understand what we mean by Pure Truth, you must first understand that the God of the Universe is even more than
you have ever hoped or even suspected. To open your
mind to a greater concept of God than you now have will
give your mind/spirit better understanding and en-
lightenment. With this understanding embedded within
you, turn to the Brotherhood who enter the earth plane to
help you eternalize (project into your life experience) the
principles we teach.

Pure Truth, that which is teamed up within each individual mind/spirit as God truth that will encourage personal potential, must be understood. No quick reading,
no abbreviated thought, no projection made in haste or
with casual inquiry will suffice here. To enter Pure Truth

**The Trilogy of Truth,* by Jean K. Foster: *The God-Mind Con-
nection,* 1987. *The Truth that Goes Unclaimed,* 1987. *Eternal Gold,*
1988. Kansas City, Uni*Sun.

within you, you must give your whole teamwork to the task. The God of the Universe stands by to give His own truth the push it needs to conceptualize it within you. The question is, however, where do you stand in this matter? The God of the Universe stands ready. The Brotherhood of God awaits your entry to them, but what will you do?

Yes, the Pure Truth, though the key to all that will bring you great happiness, will elude your grasp if you are not prepared to reach out as we have indicated.

Now—throw your old God concepts away, reader! Team up now with new God truth. Never will you depreciate the value of these new concepts of the great God of the Universe, for they will bring you the power that you may have lacked in the past to make truth really work in your lives.

Our purpose is to awaken your mind and to enter it into the great flow of Pure Truth that is now attracted to your being. It is you, remember, who attract the truth of God, not the other way around. The truth of God does not eternally chase you. You must open your mind, and thereupon the Mind of God pours through the open channel between you and this Greatness.

Teaming up with us is merely the first step in the process. Eternal goodness prevails among those in the Brotherhood. Eternal goodness eternalizes within us. Therefore, we can be trusted to open your mind fully to let the powerful thought of God Himself pour into your own mind.

This entry to God truth is what we eternalize with you right now. The open mind that you present is that which teams up with us in making a channel of truth. This channel of great wonder will unite you with what you need to become the truth in action.

Now recreate the process in your mind without our leading. Recreate the process from the point where you throw away every old concept to where a channel is built to your God-mind connection. With this in mind, you ready yourself for new truth and new teamwork.

The second thing we will discuss now is the open mind that you must bring to this exercise in teaming up with Pure Truth. An open mind is deceptively easy to operate. You say, "Yes, of course I have an open mind. I'm reading this book, aren't I?" But reading this book only plants the seeds; it does not make them grow. Yes, if you read this book, you are indeed open and receptive to Pure Truth. But the point of this book, remember, is to make the Pure Truth operate in your lifetime experience.

Tenderness is the God gift we want to give to you. This particular tenderness is not based on earth truth which wishes for tenderness and hopes it will come to each individual. Our tenderness is based on God-mind truth and is centered in the great God of the Universe. The tenderness that this wonderful God gives is totally teamed up with our every need. But when we give it to you, it is not because we feel sentimental about your being, but because we are filled to overflowing with this quality which we now want to dispense to everyone.

Perhaps this kind of tenderness seems farfetched to you who project the idea of love from one person to another. This "love" you express is not without qualification, is it? Don't you "love" one another until the other person seems to project ingratitude toward you? Even parental love bases itself on the response by the one called "child."

Now, do you see how different our tenderness based on God truth is from your tenderness based on earth truth? The first enters by way of God to overflow into our individual world and into the entire universe. Earth love enters to go to particular individuals who may lose that love unless they reciprocate in accepted ways.

The gentle presences here who go forth to enter into earth life to help those of you who want help have their tenderness from God well instated within them. They reach out to you, therefore, from their bounty, not from any personal need to be loved in return. The presences eternalize along with you what God truth is, and they will help each of you to reach the highest and best truth in this regard.

Here is the way we work to bring good to you. First, the new team goes to work within your being. You are the one to initiate the matter. We enter in response. Then we work eternally to create the open channel connection that will beam the truth from God-mind to your mind. When this happens, you will no longer resist what is truly wonderful to know. You will team up willingly every day to eternalize an open channel with God-mind, and then you will center yourself in the truth.

The eternalization that we bring to this association is that we, who eternalize what is perfect, match our beings with yours. Then we help you to team up with what we bring to you. That way you who do not understand this matter may eternalize along with those of us who do understand. Give your outstretched mind to our purpose. Present your eternalization of what is good and eternally purported to be wholly of God that we may help you to achieve it.

No entity, not you, not even those who enter this second plane of life, may team up with what the great eternalizations project unless it is understood how these projections work. For example, we have worked with this writer again and again, but she has not done all she might. This writer has, of course, teamed up to do this important writing, and she has teamed up to find the right publisher, and she enters into our guidance and into God-mind truth. But where this writer tends to get lost in the earth-mind truth is in the matter of projecting her truth into her world. This one, though entering into other good, has not put her truth to work in sufficient demonstrations.

She now eternalizes what she wants most in life, but she has not given her teamwork the thrust it needs to put those requests into the ethereal substance of the great God of the Universe. "Push into this substance," God tells her. "Put yourself into my tender care," this same

God insists. This writer enters into great tenderness but has not touched the key to **might,** to **power,** to the wonderful **energy** that God Is.

But as we write this book for the readers, we hope to change this situation so that this writer may bring her focus clearly into this matter of getting her truth into motion, into the creative thought that will eternalize whatever she most wants and needs. This writer wonders why we insist that she demonstrate **her** needs and wants, not those of the needy. But we say to her and to you, the reader, that if you cannot put your truth into motion on your own behalf, you cannot do so with the needs of others.

To read the truth we bring you is good, but to reach those in the Brotherhood is even better. Then even greater is to become the teammate with the great God of the Universe. When this third step is reached, you may reach forth your hand to take from the substance of the universe.

The eternal being that God Is, the Teammate who works with each of us—you on the earth plane, we here in this next plane—tones His Being to the same vibration that we are. That way we can communicate. But this vibratory energy, this energy that enters the earth plane when you open your mind to it, is what we call God, not just Eternal Greatness, not just Principle, not just the Entity who eternally generates truth. Teamed up within this One whom we call God are all the attributes we mention, and even more. God is the energy that pulsates through our beings to help us to be one with our Source of Light. This Source of Light is, of course, the God of the Universe.

Get into the eternal flow of the river that emanates from the Pure Truth and flows to Oneness with God. This river is your way of moving from one point to the other, from the point of understanding to the point of eternal truth expression. Get into the boat called the "Eternal Way" and row with the paddles called "Brotherhood of God." Then follow a chart to avoid the rocks and the earth that will tear the bottom out of your boat. This chart is given by those who guide you along, the Brotherhood, and it is named "Map of Eternalizations." The river itself is named "The River of No Return" because it takes you all the way to the presence of God who will then harbor your boat and provide you with all you ever want and need for yourself and for those for whom you act.

Team up, reader, with this book, with this ebb and flow that is called growth. Never let the ebbing of the river dismay you, for no temporary thwarting of your movement toward your goal will hold you permanently if you let these Brothers help you. The flow continues to take you forward into the perfection that you seek.

New Age: Passage to Purity

2

How do I survive when the earth shifts on its axis? Are there safe places? Can I expect God truth to see me safely through this period?

The New Age is not to be feared. It is, instead, to be recognized for what it is, the energy of the universe pouring through to give earth newness of life, purity, and the whole eternal concept of what is worthwhile.

The Brotherhood does not want you to create worry or undue concern about what they are about to explain. They ask only that their presentation be given a careful reading and thoughtful consideration. We will be there to help you understand it all, *the one who brings this message promises.*

The New Age is not projected as the end of the world. No! The New Age is simply better truth instated within the elements of matter in this planet you call earth. Therefore, open your minds to what we tell you, not allowing every earth truth to dominate your thinking. Instead, turn to the truth which enters you through the open channel we provide for each of you.

In the near future, as you measure time, the earth will begin the turmoil of getting new truth within itself. The truth is what brings matter into the purity which it needs to function at its highest potential. The earth must enter this period if it is to survive, and you must believe that new truth is needed to remake this earth. The old truth that mankind has depended on by way of the body of beliefs, so-called facts, and the like will no longer hold this earth together. The planet will surely let go its axis, let go its revolutions around the sun if the earth truth is heeded much longer.

The teamed up earth truth has wrung about all that is of value from this earth, but very little replenishment has occurred. The earth is losing its vitality, its eternal greatness and is losing that which holds it firmly together in the universal plan. If the earth is not revitalized soon, the earth will simply go into a void, into an emptiness which the astronomers witness here and there in the great universe. This earth you live on must enter the eternal truth within itself if it is to become the truth in expression. By this we mean that the earth will, if it teams up with better truth, become whole once again.

The earth is declining now as it goes into its throes of teeming vicissitude. The earth reflects, you see, what mankind puts forth in truth. That is why there has been so little rebuilding, so little revitalization. People have depended on what they refer to as "getting everything possible" in their lifetimes. They use the resources; they take what earth has to give. But what do they give in return? They think there is nothing to return. They think they are takers only, not givers. This philosophy is enacted by most people who live now and have lived before on this planet. The wisdom of the ages is not heeded by many. The truth of God is ignored or pushed away. Earth is used, ruptured to benefit the people who want, the people who take, the people who regard earth as theirs to use.

Earth's needs are left unmet. The earth cries out for teamed up truth to make the planet the lush garden God once created. The planet cries out for its true resources, but man says, "No way, old girl! We have our needs, you know!"

The truth that tries to make itself known pours

through, but those who know how important it is have made little progress against the overwhelming takers of the earth. Those who rise to help this earth meet derision, meet scoffing and laughter. But those who enter their wisdom in spite of this know what is needed. They team up to educate, to persuade, to open people's minds, but to little avail. The poisons pour onto the planet. The heeding of ecologists is ignored.

However, those who try (to improve earth's condition) will receive the tender blessing of these advanced spirits who teach people what is needed in the planet. Ecologists will be the first to understand the needs, and they will probably understand why the New Age is necessary if the planet is to survive. They eternalize the way this planet might be, and they see its potential even now.

The New Age is no punishment from God! The idea of punishment is erroneous. The truth here is that we bring upon ourselves whatever we truly accept. Those who better understand the way the earth must be cared for, the gentle beings who understand the custodial role of mankind, will understand the need for earth's renewal.

As for the others, well, it does not really matter, for they must undergo this change along with those who do understand. The planet, after all, includes the people who live upon it—one and all. Therefore, we bring you this new trilogy of books through this writer in order to show you all—taker and giver—how to survive in the New Age and how to bring new vitality into the eternal growth of both planet and people.

Getting new truth is, of course, the first step. The second step is becoming one with it, and the third step is the vital one—teaming up with those in the next plane who can help you to enact your truth in the world itself. These have been discussed before in the Trilogy of Truth.*

The entire thrust of our message now is to put you, the

---

*The Trilogy of Truth, by Jean K. Foster: The God-Mind Connection, 1987. The Truth that Goes Unclaimed, 1987. Eternal Gold, 1988. Kansas City, Uni*Sun.

reader, in the position of entering the New Age with the resources needed not only to survive, but to prosper. The aim of this entire series is explaining the why's of the New Age, eternalizing the truth you need to take charge of your lifetime experience, and to give you the necessary tools to accomplish what we state here. People must awaken to the renewal of the planet and its people.

Great eternalizations emerge on behalf of planet earth. Those who work with this plan eternalize the purity that earth requires to be part of the universal good. The planet must be purified! The truth is not to be quibbled over, for no planet can survive in the universe with the pollution that this planet now accumulates. Therefore, the teamwork here and there on earth now eternalizes (projects with fervor) the absolute purity of the planet. This will come about in the New Age. But attaining this purity is not what most people on earth will readily team up with. Why? Well, to attain purity, the earth must receive new ingestion.

I stopped the transmission to ask for further explanation.

The ingestion takes place much in the same way your own bodies ingest nourishment. The earth is fed the magnificent truth of wisdom of the great God of the Universe, that Principle of Good, that Teammate of Power, that Great Gift of Purity itself, to ready it for the ingestion. The truth is spread all over the planet. We do this thing now along with others both in the earth plane and in advanced planes. Then will come the giant turn of the earth on its axis. When this event takes place, the truth is ingested within this ball of creativity. As the earth stirs itself with this mighty surge, the truth eternalizes or projects itself into the material substance.

Nothing to fear in this, those of you who cringe and gasp. Nothing to worry over when this giant turn comes! You, the entities who will be walking this planet, will scurry here and there to survive, but eternalizations within you based on the mighty eternal truth will sustain your every need. Why worry, then?

The earth will shudder in the beginning of the travail,

as a mother shudders at the signs of giving birth. Then comes the painful thrust as the "baby" is born, and the earth will turn to respond to a different point in the heavens.

Again I asked for explanation.

The earth will give itself over to the natural process of renewal. Do not enter into fearful thoughts. Enter into great anticipation of the perfection to come. Enter into the Pure Truth which will provide you with what your body needs to survive this upheaval. When you have done this, what problem can you have?

We know some hate change of any kind, even change to their betterment. To these the upheaval will cause a period of grief. Some of you will eternalize suffering and death, perhaps. Some of you will see hurt, a time of awful circumstances. To you we say that you will receive what you expect.

But we say to those who announce to your being that God-mind truth will save the day and that the truth will project through you and your Teammate, God, that the approaching time is a great adventure which you will enter into with every joy that earth can provide. This kind of joy is possible because you are clothed in the truth of God which transforms appearances into the reality that you are able to perceive.

I asked for an example of how God-mind truth will save the day.

Those of you who perceive with true sight will provide housing, food, clothes. You will eternalize so clearly that no want, no need will be ignored. Those of you who decide now to be the truth eternalizers will lead others who weaken in resolve. You will be as the good shepherd who tends to his flock. The wonder will team up within you to project into your world, and others will flock to you for understanding.

New gentle thoughts will pervade the planet, and those who warred will find nothing to go to war over. They may posture and stamp their feet, but to no avail. The boundaries of countries will change, and some countries will

disappear altogether. The truth will go into action to provide wholesome environment, and those who walk the
earth will weep with the greatness of what they see, what
they experience and what they enjoy.

Nothing that enters the universal consciousness of
those on the planet will besmirch what has been wrought
there. They will be caught up in God truth to the point
that no truth other than God truth has any power. They
will turn to this greatness as to their Source, for that is
what the eternalizations are all about. People project the
good that they want and the truth of God goes into
manifestation. They assist in the process, and with God
eternally with them, the earth will prosper and thrive as it
has not thrived since the last eternal truth brought the
upheaval that renewed it.

Yes, the earth has renewed itself before—many times,
in fact. This planet eternalized its goodness to bring it
into the perfection that God wanted. This wisdom
projected into the earth itself, and those who walked the
earth tried to keep what they had. But so many did not
understand the greatness that they eternalized it as the
truth which projected mankind as the better gods, the
ones who could take charge. Slowly the idea of the Users
developed. The few who eternalized themselves as the
Givers to the earth became outnumbered and were overcome by the force of the Users.

We come again to a time when this earth must renew itself. The Users have again overcome the Givers in num-
bers, but the truth of what the earth needs has even
swept over the Users. They open themselves to the need
for purity, and therefore, they enter the New Age with the
idea of teamwork with the goal of planet renewal.

The reason we express the New Age as entering into
the Purification Period is that you must realize there is
nothing fearsome in this event. Those who would tell you
that the end of the world is at hand are wrong. Those who
tell you the hour of judgment is now upon you are also
wrong. The time for the optimum energy of the universal
thought, which we know is God Himself, is now enacting

the wholeness concept that is part of the God nature. Wholeness is an integral part of God; therefore, that which is of God, and this planet is of this Universal Greatness, must become whole!

What is there to fear? That event is just the eternalization of what God Is—whole. Truth materializes into tremendous energy which returns earth to that which it must express! What we tell you is true, not a story about God's judgment!

You are spirit. The God of the Universe is Spirit. We in the other planes of life are spirit. And all of us are in the same vibration. Earth is material; your body is material; the universe has many material bodies. The spirit, however, is the prime mover of all materiality. The spirit is the only truth that survives in permanent fashion. The earth would enter into a void without the truth which sustains it! The body you inhabit would lie down and die if the spirit that inhabits it did not pour truth into it! Herein lies the plan of the universe!

Participate in this plan by acknowledging spirit as reality! Then team up with what will truly help you day by day, event by event, even to the turning of the earth on its axis!

Now reach into your being, deep within your spirit self. Tune your being into the words we speak. Gently settle your thoughts until there is peace within you. Ready? If not, wait until you feel the peace settling, settling over you, through you.

The Brotherhood offered the following meditation:

TRUTH THAT TURNS THE WORLD

Within your spirit self is the bright light of the God of the Universe. This bright light turns to its Teammate, the One Who Is that Source of Light. The entity that you are, your reality or spirit self, wants to join its light with that Great Light. Therefore, you, that gentle light that turns hopefully toward its Source, open your mind, your very core, to what the Source of Light Is.

Say to yourself: "I AM the gentle being who turns to the Source of all Light. I open myself to all that this Source IS." Wait while you think on this statement. Then continue. "That which IS, that which teams up with me, that which holds every truth worth having, is the One whom I now give my own light to." Wait while you think on these words.

The Source of Light moves toward you because you are now irresistible. You are the openness that this Source must fill with its Being, its Wisdom, its Eternal Gifts. Think on these words. Team up with the idea. Turn resolutely toward that Light which is, of course, the God of the Universe. This team is now instated within you—the lights merge—the wisdom imparts itself to you through the open channel now formed between you and that Source. Energy pours through and teams up with your body. The joy and hope of teamwork manifests in the body too. The entity that you are—your spirit self—enters your own New Age where you await the coming earth renewal.

The words in themselves are not magic, of course. Only you, the spirit self, may make them what they appear to be—the way to unite with the great God of the Universe. We, the Brotherhood of God, those who exist in this plane to help you in the earth plane, only show you the way. We cannot enact it. We cannot lead you there. We cannot push you. The key to all truth is your openness to it.

Therefore, team up with what you now know is best for your soul, what is best for your body, too. The entity who you are reaches out for what is best, what is worthy, what is positive. You recognize this urge within you. You want to satisfy it by putting the Pure Truth of God into your own being.

The chapter will end on this note, we think. It gives positive truth to each reader that you may understand what is ahead, what is the truth.

Getting Your House in Order

3

If I abandon earth truth, how can I survive in this material world?

The only way to evaluate your truth is to put it to work in your life experience. When you see it performing your drumbeat, you will know how to evaluate its worth.

The truth of earth-mind provides much that enters your life experience each and every day. "They say ....." indicates that whatever follows is indeed a truth which must be given its honor and recognition. Yes, "They say ....." provides a person with an unnamed authority who is undoubtedly from earth-mind truth. People use that team of "experts" regularly—the "they" of the earth plane.

Nothing projects authority in people's minds more than that particular beginning to some so-called truth or other. The words may not be anything more than some half truth that people have come to accept as truth. Yet, they repeat it as a so-called valuable and worthy statement. What are you to do? Enter into it because it is generally encouraged by reputable people whom you know to be well-meaning?

No! You must reckon with the difference between what is real God truth and what is merely the "accepted way" of the earth-mind collection of facts, truths, half truth and outright lies!

Pay the eternal value that is required to get eternal truth! By this we mean to reckon with the good coin of the realm—the coin of truth that enters you through your mind, your spirit self, your reality. The body self is only the entity in which you move, not the whole and perfect you. Therefore, reject whatever comes through those who want to help, those who are well meaning. Reject whatever thought that others give you full blown "for your own good." The only way to know what is right and true for you is to receive it firsthand, not secondhand.

A well-meaning friend may inadvertently corrupt your thinking. A helpful parent may turn you away from your true purpose in life. The entire teamwork of earth may give you all they know and understand only to thwart your real purpose in coming to this planet earth. Better truth than earth provides is found in the universal truth which speaks directly to your soul.

The truth from the God of the Universe never disappoints you, never leads you into discouragement, never holds you responsible for failure, never tells you that you are evil, never holds you bound to that which teams up with what hurts you in any way. "This is impossible!" you cry out. "Nothing is supposed to be that good! We who live upon the face of this earth must suffer."

If the words above relate to you in any way, you are the one we speak to now. The Truth of God, the Pure Truth, the Truth that enters to overcome all the anxieties that earth truth produces, the Truth that enters into your life with power, teamwork, and results—this is the truth we speak of now. No one who enters to receive this Pure Truth will get the gross product of nothingness. No one will receive the teamwork that results in anything except the building of your being into that which in your heart you want most to be.

Therefore, we seek today to enter into partnership with

those of you who find earth truth disappointing, to say the least. We plead today to give you the perfect truth that will turn your life into one of joyous living. Why hesitate? Why play with the subject until you have no enthusiastic response to us at all?

Now—let us suppose you give some kind of affirmative answer. You may say, "Well, go ahead. Give me that truth!" or you may team up wholeheartedly to open your mind to us. But at any rate, we will be glad for any response that means that you are, at least, considering the worth of what we say here.

Put your mind to work—not your brain, per se, but your mind. This mind is not of earth at all; it is of spirit! The mind turns its face to what is reality, what is the truth of its being. Therefore, when you turn your mind to our message, it must respond, for it knows its Source. That Source is that body of spirit that enters the universal teamwork to provide you with whatever you want and need—if these are for your good. The Principle will not apply if you turn your mind to acquiring power over others. That sort of goal turns to earth-mind truth.

The God of the Universe, that Being which is Principle, that Being which is Law or Lord of all, that Being which is the entire Gift you seek—this God is the one we introduce to overcome the truth of earth.

"Why hasn't this God stepped forth and brought the earth into submission?" you ask. Did we say God was the Dictator Who Rules All Creation? No! God has power, but His power is for good, not for the purpose of ruling others. The Principle of God is that which pours forth the opportunity, that which rises above the threadbare truth of earth, that which offers but never forces itself upon those who are the offshoots of His Being.

Take the word of this Brotherhood who are the advanced spirits who enter your earth plane to help you to understand who you are, who God is, what your purpose is on the earth plane, and how to use truth to bring your life into sublime eternal good. The teamwork we will provide will help you to link with your truth that will come to you from the greatness of the Communicator God.

There are those among you who regard God as a vast silence. There are those among you who team up with the idea that God discourages any thought of being practical and helpful in your day by day life. There are many who persist in the thought that God is more interested in suffering than He is in the other side of the coin—the teamwork that will bring you joy, positive influences, tenderness and good gifts.

Why would God be uncommunicative? Why would the vastness we try to eternalize be silent? Why would the God we tell you of want to be shrouded in mystery? Why, you might better ask, would mankind put limits on God? The teamwork we give you tells you that God is here for you; you can open your mind to receive His words, His greatness, His gifts, or you can choose to pray with the thought of a great gulf between you and God—which is the way most people pray.

The Universal Presence we call God is eternal, yes! That means merely that He is forever. That He is personal is true only if you understand who you are. You are the truth in expression here on earth. You, the offshoot or child of God, give your truth to the earth in your own way and by whatever means you employ. Then you return here (to the next plane of life) to evaluate the whole experience. The truth you expressed (in your lifetime) may not have been much, and when you evaluate it, you mourn your lost opportunity! But then you go over the many, many lifetimes you have lived only to see how the truth has gone astray too many times!

Now we say to you, the time has come in the eternal quest for your perfection to team up with the growth plan you went to earth to enact. There is no time left to eternalize with the earth-mind truth. The eternal truth teams up with the way the earth must renew itself. You, the man or the woman who wants to have Truth that will provide you with your every need and will project your goodness into the world around you, may achieve this goal.

Therefore, put yourself into our teamwork. We, who want only for you to express the goodness that Truth from God brings, want to help you. We stand by now to receive your request, your open mind, your willingness to pursue Pure Truth.

Give your openness to our openness. We reach out to you in this thought. Gentle presences go toward you now, gentle presences who only seek your perfect expression of good. These presences are those advanced spirits who enter into this work with the encouragement of God Himself. Needs that you project to us will be met as you allow us to counsel with you. We will help you to solve your problems, meet your questions with answers, enter into the sublime way of life rather than enter into a lifetime where your energy ebbs away. Gentle presences give their truth to you now.

The one who stepped forth, one of the gentle presences described above, began.

The writer of this book opened her mind to our presence, and then we helped her make contact by much practice in writing. Her being resisted, as we have told about in other books. But when she determined that we wanted only her own good, she relaxed and followed our suggestions to help her to communicate through writing. But now she can communicate through her mind without the need of writing. There are other ways besides this way.

One may, if the sight is clear, see the words pass through his mind. He may read the words as he reads a letter. Others may, if they have the ears for it, listen to the voice within. But the most common form of our communication is the writing which propels the fingers into letters and the letters into words.

In other books by this writer the method is given in detail.* Here we will merely say that if you wish to have this communication, find a way, for now is the time to get

---

*The Trilogy of Truth, by Jean K. Foster: *The God-Mind Connection*, 1987. *The Truth that Goes Unclaimed*, 1987. *Eternal Gold*, 1988. Kansas City, Uni*Sun.

your house in order. By "house" we mean the place of your thinking, the inner temple where you team up with the Teammate of the Universal Truth.

Gentle presences work with this writer every day. Though she receives well, she still must work with her truth to express it in her lifetime experience. But we can speak with her as brother to brother, and in that way we counsel with her. She can now team up with the greatness of the Communicator Himself who offers her the entry into God-mind where she receives the exact truth her own soul needs.

This exact truth is what each reader needs. The writer's truth, with which she fills notebooks, is still her own, and hers will not match what you need. But the great Communicator knows the individual soul's needs and provides that Truth of His which is especially helpful to you. What more could you want, reader? By teaming up with the Brotherhood of God here in this second plane of life, you can receive counseling and help in your daily living, but best of all you can receive the absolute Pure Truth for your own soul!

No entity who touches this Source will ever meet with hopelessness or depression. The entity who realizes the value in our teamwork will progress in this lifetime with such speed and clarity of thought that he will soon not be the same person at all, but he will be more vigorous, more gentle, more powerful, more tender. His experiences will inspire wonder, and his life will give others cause for getting whatever it is that he has. That is the way to provide a witness in the world. Be! No amount of telling, no amount of giving, no amount of providing people with their benefits will bring them to the powerful God self who can take care of himself. But the one who masters truth in expression will indeed solve the problems of earth life.

Yes, the truth we speak of will project no hurt, no deprivation, no cause for alarm. The Pure Truth only expresses the good that people truly want and need. In the New Age of which we speak, the people will provide for their needs by way of their truth. How will anyone survive, let alone prosper, if he only has earth truth before him? Their needs will be overwhelming.

Water to drink—where will that come from? The way to provide for bodily needs? How would you manage with reliance on earth truth? The earth will be turned upside down, stirred up, reconditioned. Though this is needed, people will not appreciate the turmoil. They will suffer unless they not only have the Truth of the God of the Universe within them, but the understanding of how to express that truth.

We want you to live well. We want you to be with the eternalization that all is well no matter what the appearance. The reality that you must learn to enter into your every thought will be that which will provide your needs. Now, give your openness to us, to this team of Brothers who want to provide you with the tools of understanding

The entire thrust of our message in this chapter is to right the wrong thinking that will lead you to refuse a better way of life. This truth we present to you as Pure Truth that comes through God-mind will team up with whoever you are in your reality. It will bring your reality into its perspective of who it is—that is, who you are—and who is the prime mover of the universe. This is our good message we enter here through the channel of this writer who now eternalizes it into a form that you can read.

Now we wrest out the evil that your earth-mind thoughts produce. Evil enters only if you let it, not because it is "out there somewhere." Evil is of the power that your mind produces when it focuses wholly on earth-mind truth. Evil is what preachers say that God fights. But God's nature is not militant. God's nature is one of Pure Truth which holds no evil thought. By its very absence of evil thought, it negates it of power. And that is also possible for you to do.

What more could you want of us than this offer of putting the open channel into your being that you may get your own absolute truth through the Perfection which is

NEW EARTH—NEW TRUTH

God-mind? What more could you want than the promise we readily give that you can enter into the God truth with such greatness that your every need is met and your every good is expressed?

Team up with us now.

Truth Worth Going After

4

What will God-mind truth bring to my life that earth-mind truth cannot bring?

God-mind truth is not impractical in the manner of pretty ideas that a person binds and puts with other books he reads once and then stands in public view. This kind of truth must be more than a one time thing. It must give each person total control over his life.

This truth is based on the principles and the law of God. These great ideas generate what we know as the entering optimum energy that unites with whatever the individual has need of. This energy becomes—yes, *becomes*—that which the individual with understanding wants to produce. Teaming up the energy with the eternalization, a good need or desire, constitutes the optimum expression which we here want you there to put to use.

In order to understand the thrust of this chapter, the advanced spirit from the Brotherhood gives a comprehensive background on this matter of truth. If the reader is to make a choice regarding which truth he wants, he must get the full picture.

The earth-mind truth rushes to fill the vacuum that most people present to the universe. No one who plays with earth truth will be free of its effects. No one who opens his mind to "what people say" or to what is pre-

NEW EARTH—NEW TRUTH

sented through self-proclaimed earthly guides can ever team up with the perfection of you—that reality called spirit or mind.

The truth that earth teaches is compounded daily by those who keep turning to it, thus giving it momentum. Those who give their thoughts to this accumulation of what people tend to believe will never rise to their top potential. Those who become famous may team up with a variety of truths that receive their energy from earth-mind. But no one will know greatness except from God truth.

But we do not judge each person. We enter to help, not judge, not threaten, not even to provoke you into rising to your potential. The Brotherhood only wants to help you to open your mind to the God of the Universe, the One who has the only truth worth having. This God is not stingy with the truth, though one might think so when the earth teams up with so much of what is poor, ineffectual truth. Also, this God is not One who gives only to deserving people.

It is true that the rain falls upon the just and the unjust, no matter how disappointing this is to those self-proclaimed truth-tellers on earth. God does not discriminate. He provides for everyone, but few have ears to hear or eyes to see. That is what this chapter is all about. Those who wander in the earth plane unsure and full of judgment on others enter into the least of their potential. Why? They team up with negative thoughts and negative opinions. This state of mind produces no benefits for the individual nor for those in his world.

Therefore, in order to reach forth your hands to team up with the Brotherhood, to open your mind to the thought that God-mind is attainable, you must entertain no judgment of others or of God. Yes, some people do judge God. They are forever saying, "The teaming up of God with man takes place IF man does such and such with his life."

Here is an example. The poor truth of earth proclaims that mankind is entered in the teamwork of the devil. Therefore, unless mankind does certain things, he cannot

26

meet God. God will draw apart, this thought persists. What a lot of trash! God never draws apart from you. The thought in your mind may hold this view, but in reality God is there just as you are there ready to interact. If you turn your back on the Greatness, on the Perfection, then you enter into the eternalization that God is only a Being that is out there somewhere.

But those who take the idea to their hearts and make it theirs that God only wants to give good gifts will get their rewards. Yes, God only wants to give, not to punish, not to stand back while you crawl to Him, not to watch you suffer or become a wretched and poor individual who waits to be forgiven. Wherever did you get the idea that God is less than the "All in all"?

Gentle thoughts rise to the surface of your mind, thoughts that teach you that God's nature is kind, tempered with overwhelming generosity. Will you run and hide? Or will you stand there wreathed in smiles, your arms outstretched? Give these gentle thoughts sway over your mind; do not put them firmly away because they are too wonderful for you!

The writer of this book enters her own thoughts on this matter. This one wants God's goodness and reaches out for it. This one wants even more than she now sees. The key to her desire is only this—that her being may receive as much as she can open her mind to. Whenever she thinks that God is limited in some way, **she** puts the limits upon Him. Why can't God rise above her getting better truth? Because He can only interact to the point where each person has become open to an ever-expanding concept of God.

Yes, the key to increasing your ability to receive good gifts from God is to open your mind to the perfection that is unending! It is not the gifts themselves that are in short supply. The gifts from God enter as fast as you can open your mind to receive them. That's the way it is. Your being has the key, your being that operates as spirit/mind.

No, these thoughts that come through us to the writer

and thus to the paper are not unchristian. What, after all, is Christ? Why, the Christ is that channel from mankind to God-mind. The Christ is the Communicator that people want to use in order to put their lifetimes in good working order.

Those readers who do not think of themselves as Christian may think this book is turning to the everlasting proposition that each person must get salvation in the one manner provided by churches. No! We say, No, No, No! The way to God is not a far thing. God and man are as close as twins in the womb. What could be closer? The idea of any earthly pontificator denying you contact with God is ridiculous! Therefore, whatever your thinking, whatever your background in religion, open your mind to **New Thinking.**

The figure that most Christian people consider is the one who enacted his lifetime experience as Jesus of Nazareth. This entity, this great spirit who enacted his truth perfectly on the earth plane, did not go there to begin a religious movement. He went to bring **new thought.** But even this entity who was the personification of God's own truth could not persuade mankind to give up their idolatrous ways.

The writer of this book winces! She wonders if we are becoming harsh. But the message that we give here enters through the open channel from God-mind itself. Therefore, it is not opinion, readers, it is the eternal truth that pours through this channel. Getting the everlasting truth is what we project here for you, for this kind of truth will bring you teamwork with the God of the Universe, no less! This is our teamwork—that which works with you to bring you into this eternal truth!

Now we want to express the tenderness that is abundant among this Brotherhood for you, the readers of this book. Perhaps you are astounded by much that you read. Perhaps you reject much of what you find here. The Brotherhood understands your reluctance. Yes, they, too, wanted once to team up with earth truth. They, too, lived in earth to express their identities as people like you.

They, too, made the truth work for them—at times. They, too, went to earth many, many times to try to get their growth plan enacted. They understand your dilemma. They tenderly wish you well in your own mental turmoil as you present these thoughts to your inmost being for better expression.

How the open truth tries to reach you! If you only knew the efforts on this side on your behalf! If you only knew how the Tender Teammate, the Supreme Thought, tries to express through you! If you understood this fully, you would think your life transformed into one of greatness immediately, for you would open to all the great potential of the universal truth.

How weak is the earth truth by comparison to the Supreme Truth. How everlastingly poor are the values of the truth which emanates from earth-mind. Yet the people continue to express this weak, inferior and awful truth. Why? The reason is, readers, that they team up with what has always been. They feel more acceptable to their peers if they get their truth as they do. Where is the advancement this way? Where is the movement toward perfection?

Be your potential. This is our message in a nutshell. Why settle for less? Be that which you came to earth to be, not that which enters here only to eternalize the same old earth truth yet one more time. This greatness of the God of the Universe wants to express through you, but the key is to open your mind to this thought and let it eternalize within you.

Can you see it happening? Can you eternalize this Greatness entering your life? It is better than any happy experience you have ever had. Yes, it overthrows all that you have ever thought wonderful! How can this be? Because you, reader, are eternal yourself, and you respond to anything eternal with great fervor. The things of earth, while momentarily satisfying, cannot give you overwhelming tenderness, overriding satisfaction and perfect goodness that enhances your life.

We have made a case for eternal truth, have we not?

NEW EARTH—NEW TRUTH

Probably all of you say it would be wonderful to have that kind of truth. How many, however, will accept this eternal truth? Will you reject what has been opinionated in the churches, in the philosophies? Will you strike out anew to build your own spirit self with truth? Remember, the truth that will bring you to your potential is not exactly that which will bring another to his potential. Therefore, do not judge others. The truth that enhances you must be understood to be your own, not your brother's. Therefore, let your brother go his way in finding truth, and you go yours.

The thought we want to open to your mind is that you have the opportunity to master the truth of the optimum energy. This thought may not mean much to you at first, but when you put it to work in your life, you will eventually have control of your world. The optimum energy is that which expresses to the utmost.

I suggested that an example might be helpful.

The only way to understand what we speak of is to try it. An example is just that—an example! If we show you what one person has done, perhaps you would say, "Why, I have no need of expressing such a thing," and you would be unimpressed. The thing that you personally want to express now is what will impress you and make you understand what it will mean in your life to express this truth to the utmost.

Give yourself an opportunity to take charge, not only of yourself, but the needs you see around you. Entering into this New Age will not be easy if you only have the earth truth to rely on. But if you turn to God truth, the truth of the universe, the eternal truth, then you will take charge and produce whatever it is that you need.

Some may think of riches at this point. You may think in terms of winning the lottery or producing the equivalent amount of dollars. But what we speak of is greater than that idea, greater by far. The truth that will free you of physical concerns, the truth that will eternalize whatever your body needs, is what we speak of now. The New Age will require much in the way of skills. Therefore, you who are not prepared to take care of yourself, you who have not eternalized the tools or the resources, may now learn to take hold of this situation with optimum energy that will express all that you may need.

Give your being its good by turning to the channel that affords you the opportunity to open your mind to the great God-mind. There you will learn; there you will team up with the knowledge, theunderstanding, the tender expression of gentle presences, as well as those attributes that make it possible for you to be the perfect truth in expression.

Ready? Then read on.

Meet the Tender Presences

5

How can advanced spirits help me to live successfully now and in the New Age?

The tender presences who team up with you in the earth plane help you in everything that concerns you. These presences enter your plane with no thoughts of judgment, or criticism or forming opinions of you. They only represent the God of the Universe in whom they move and have their beings.

By opening your mind to these presences who come upon request—yours or someone else's request on your behalf—you will center your being and become one who enters the presence of God. So that the presences may team up with you better, we give this discussion of their work, their presence in the earth plane, and their good teamwork that will make all the difference in the attainment of your growth plan.

Now pay attention here. These presences, who only want to help you, are teamed up with our Brotherhood. They specialize in helping those who live in the earth plane. These presences water the seeds within you, and they realize their own goals when you realize yours. Therefore, when you open your mind to their beings, you open your mind to what is for your highest and best. No one will enjoin you to enact wrong thoughts or wrong truths. No tender presence will ever order you about. No!

The way to be aware of their presence is to team up with encouraging forces you perceive with your inner self. Then acknowledge their presence, their teamwork with the God of the Universe. You will then be part of their thought perception of what is helpful to you.

Nothing that eternalizes when these gentle presences enter will lead you to anything that is considered base or gross. They bring only that which will center you in the God self of your own being. In that quiet place there is nothing that even suggests imperfection.

No, dear reader, you have nothing to fear and everything to gain by putting these gentle presences into the teamwork of your being. These who work with you are the teammates who specialize in your own growth pattern. They eternalize what you yourself eternalize, and you know their great help in accomplishing whatever your plan holds. Not only will you be delighted, but so will the gentle presences, for you are their project, so to speak.

Those who want no part of these gentle presences do not know what they turn away! People who consider the intimacy that these spirits have with each person may reject them out of hand. But if you who team up with them will tell others how successful you are with these helpers who enter into your soul work, then perhaps you might persuade others. But it is hard to persuade people of anything that they reject out of hand. The very lack of rationale means that prejudice is deep. There may be reasons why some think of tender presences as those who take over. Perhaps the rejecter, in another lifetime, was full of powerful plans to control others. He may keep that old suspicion that he himself engendered.

Put no thought into yourself that there could be anyone in this Brotherhood who would want to rule your spirit. What would be the need? The old story line about selling your soul to the devil is fantasy. There is no devil, first of all. There is no powerful spirit who can say "yea" or "nay" to what becomes of your soul. There is total free will on this matter. You decide, not another.

Be assured that the perfection your soul seeks—and make no mistake about it, it does seek perfection—is made easier by these tender presences. They become what you cannot become—those who can view your lifetime with the perspective that sees both backward and forward. "Backward" means to former lifetimes, and "forward" means to the goals set in your growth plan. These presences wander the earth seeking employment, for their work is to help. They who have the authority to help you only await your open mind and your invitation.

The God of the Universe provides this perfect plan to enable his beloved spirit entities to return to His Light. He says to these graduate students of His, "Go into the earth and seek those who want to reunite with me. Team up with them to enable them to hasten their reunion." Then they go out. By now there are millions and millions of these tender presences. They hover constantly right there in your world ready to help anyone who wants to advance his understanding in his truth. The presences operate with concern, gentleness, tenderness, and they attach their teamwork to whoever wants this wonderful help.

The tender presences team up to train you to put the wonderful truth you receive to work in your earthly lifetime experience. If you who know how to give good gifts to your own children understand your reasons for doing so, then you will understand why the tender presences do this with you. The realization of your relationship is what we speak of. The child you have is much loved, much appreciated, much enveloped with your tenderness, right? That kind of love in the earth plane is well understood. Therefore, if you understand this earthly relationship, you can understand why the tender presences, filled as they are with the Teammate's tenderness, want to give their good help to you who have such great needs.

Perhaps we stand now at an impasse. We know how to give, how to be the good teammates that you so desperately need, but you may have no realization of your own needs. What can we do to get ourselves into the proper relationship so that our teamwork can progress? What can we do to put you into the entire open thought that will give you the answer to your problems?

Will you work on this matter? The tender presences are here for you. How can you open to them, how can you enter into a perfect alliance? We hope you think that you can team up with no trouble. The opinion here is that once you know of these presences, you will hasten to make use of their services. Isn't that a reasonable assumption?

Be the open minds, the open entities, the open individuals who never turn away a good idea! Why reject what you have not tried? Turn your mind to the center of your being, to the perfection that resides within, the oneness that tries to express as God truth. It is here you know what is true, what is good. Wait in this inner temple to enter into the teamwork with these who now approach.

Beings who turn in this way to the tender presences eternalize the greatest truth possible; they open their minds and thus open their power centers. Herein lies the way to great expression, you see. Herein lies the way to become the truth in expression that eternalizes as God truth. Pure Truth emerges in the earth plane as your potential. What more could you want than to express your potential?

The presences give their gentleness into your life. This is how you know they are there. The tenderness that each longs to have expressed will be within you. The gentle ones, these tender presences, these who understand your deepest yearnings, will give your being that which it longs for.

Needs that you have hidden even from your own being will rise to the surface of your thinking. You may say to yourself, "How I have longed for perfect understanding of myself!" Or you may admit that the tender expression of love has been missing both in the receiving and in the giving. But once these tender presences enter, the team-work will produce these qualities within you—the ones that keep you satisfied and the ones that you can now express.

This is how it works. First the tender presences, who are full to overflowing with their goodness, their mercy, their endearing qualities of the positive influence of the God of the Universe, pour forth from these gifts into your own domain. These who have let themselves be filled to overflowing now give to you from this overflow. They expect nothing in return. What could you give that they might need? You may know love, but do you have an abundance? You may have gentleness in your nature, but is it always there? What is the overflow that your being manifests?

The truth manifests within your being, and you must understand how it works if you are to accept this goodness. Tender presences are not the vague illusions some may think they are. They are not the positive thought that comes and then goes. They are not the proof of your best thought at the moment. No! They are real. They are advanced spirits who reside in this next plane of life where the reality of you will one day come. These who work among you bringing you the great spiritual gifts will empty these upon you as you acknowledge their reality. We are taking for granted here that you already understand what your own reality is.

The point is that you may have these quite satisfying gifts if you acknowledge the ones who bring them to you. Why is recognition necessary? Because recognition opens your mind to the possible relationship between you and them. If you cannot recognize these presences as real, you cannot open your mind to the gifts they bring. Reality is that which you bring into your own mind, not something told to you or held in the mind of others. Team up with the presences because they are real, not because we tell you of them.

Now arrange yourself in a comfortable position. Team up the best you can with your inner reality, the being who is your reality. Acknowledge its presence within your body. Then wait until you feel comfortable.

Here is the way to release your reality and to open to these who want to help you day by day, hour by hour, minute by minute.

MEDITATION

Place your being, your spirit self, in total awareness. The body self may want to relax to the point of becoming almost unnoticed. When you have done this, get into the open channel that connects you with God-mind truth.

Now let your mind relax to receive your truth.

When you have the truth you need, gently release your being to walk in this plane. Gently, now. Do not tread with harsh steps!

Your being wants help to put the truth it has just received into the perfection it needs in order to generate certain changes in your life. Ready? The gentle ones, the tender presences, wait there to assist, to encourage and to elevate you. Just think into this place, "I am ready for your help. Here I am."

The tender ones now step forth gladly to mingle themselves with your being. They welcome you to this teamwork, to this partnership. They team up with you, your truth, your whole identity to help you to become whatever it is, in truth, that you want to be. You will not be alone now in your soul work; you will not try and fail. You will try with their support and win! Tenderly they approach, and tenderly they work with you.

These who work with you will be available from now on. Your mere thought of them will bring them near. Your mere thought of their help in your life will bring that help. But when you want to be private, they, too, will be private. They who come to help will never push nor strain. They who offer you their friendship beyond all ideal relationships will never throw themselves into your lives nor take over. Their very names—tender presences—tell you that they indeed enter only when you team up with them.

Now you have true friends, true entities who will never forsake or turn away from you. Those who want perfect understanding now have it. Put your mind at rest.

Use the meditation whenever you have need of it. Soon you will have developed your own, and it will be briefer than words. The secret way you will develop with your tender presences will bring them immediately. You will say the word, think a certain thought, open your mind to their presence, and lo, your partnership is at work. Team up, dear reader, team up with those who hover there waiting for you. Turn to them to receive the special help that will bring you into the truth that pours out from God-mind just for you. And when it pours forth, these who help will show you how to become one with that truth and then how to make it work in your own life.

The Choice is Yours

6

Can I manifest what is good for others as well as for myself?

Now is the moment of reckoning! Now is the time of truth! What will you enter into your minds in the way of permanent truth, the God truth we have been talking of?

Your choice is now called for; your being is challenged. Will you put forth the effort that calls for your best work?

Teaming up with those tender presences we told you of in the last chapter is your first step toward the goal of reaching your potential, your oneness with all that is of the God of the Universe. Have you taken this step?

If the answer is "yes," you may team up with the whole message we present in this chapter. If the answer is "no," you may not even understand this message. We who are bringing this message to you know the value of decision. Without decision there is no movement toward any goal, whether it be the goal of earth truth or the goal of God truth. But make no mistake about it, we in this plane who advise you in this matter are presenting information to help you perfectly understand all that enters you through God-mind, not earth-mind.

Enter into this chapter with a firm decision to unite with those who hover nearby to open your mind and open your eyes. This writer went through this process in the beginning. With every good intention, she entered into our communication, but we insisted on her open mind, her open eyes. She grew impatient; she wanted to move on. But there is no moving forward until the individual is open in his approach to God-mind truth.

Tune your being into those who stand by to help you. Quiet your body. Quiet your mind. Know the presence of those you cannot see with earthly eyes, those who can help you to make a profound difference in your life. Now then, you are ready to move forward.

Never think that everyone in the earth plane is practicing an awareness of tender presences. You may feel that you plow a new field all alone. You may think that no one else has ever done what you do. But it is not true, of course. You may not meet anyone else, at first, who is doing what you are doing. But here is the heart of the matter. The will to make this contact is all that is important. Sharing with others in the earth plane may only hold you back at first. The way to progress rapidly is to keep this matter to yourself, to grow in understanding and to grow in performance. Finally, you can share with others because you will not weaken in resolve if met with apprehension or with ridicule.

Turn your being into the fullness of perfection. Turn your being into all that is the total freedom. Turn your being into perfect greatness, perfect power, perfect wholeness. These qualities define your potential. Yes, these and even more.

New thoughts that arise within you need to be acted upon. The writer acted upon a new thought "to write a tome."* This thought caused her amazement at first, but she persevered even though she felt foolish and totally inexperienced. The writer grew in confidence, however, and now writes with the assurance that she is communicating directly with the God-mind source. But it was not so in the beginning. This entity had to question, to

---

*The Trilogy of Truth, by Jean K. Foster: The God-Mind Connection, 1987. The Truth that Goes Unclaimed, 1987. Eternal Gold, 1988. Kansas City, Uni*Sun.

doubt, to hesitate, to think things over. You, too, may need to do these things.

But once you make the decision to move forward to God truth, to put your being in the eternalization of the open channel where you contact God-mind truth, you will be off and running toward the goal of your spirit. You can expect to change, but every change will be for the better, rest assured of this truth. The thoughts you will wrest from the open channel will thrill you and speak to the very heart of you. These thoughts will open your eyes to the potential that you came to earth to express.

Be generous with what you learn to do. Give to others as you give to yourself. This suggestion does not mean to order others around or to operate as one who knows all. No! The generous act is just that—generous. When you use truth to provide for yourself, use it also to provide for the entire world around you. That way, when the New Age comes, you will be a center of providence—a center for giving, a center for healing.

This book and two others yet to come will be the textbooks which will open possibilities to you. Therefore, use them to put wisdom within you so that you will be a walking textbook, a walking performance, a demonstrator of every Godly truth. That way you will bring help into this next age.

Not all will be able to do this, of course, but the goal we have now is to get thousands upon thousands around the planet to enter into this perfect plan. Thoroughly discourage any earth truth thought that declares the impossibility of what we say. The earth truth tries to wet down most great ideas, you know. The way to greatness is through rising to God truth, not pouring cold water upon it.

Now—ready yourself for the first eternalization we want you to learn. This eternalization is the one you will need immediately in the New Age. Team up with us now. Team up also with those tender presences who work only with your own being. The way will be made clear through their help. Believe us.

Put aside all preconceived ideas of how to get material things. Here is the first step. The first thought that comes to your mind—go to the store and buy what you want—is to be put aside. So, too, are the thoughts of creating things you want. Have you cleared your mind of those old thoughts? Have you opened your mind to new thought, to the perfect answer to whatever you might need or want?

Let your tender presences meditate with you. Use their wisdom that knows how to express itself to your own being. Quietly absorb what they tell you, and when you have truly become one with new thinking, read further.

Now we proceed. Those who come to express this subject to you specialize in how to demonstrate the physical necessities of life —good nourishment and good shelter. These who now enter will tell it to you in their own way.

For a few moments there was no communication, no trembling energy that wanted expression. Then, abruptly, the next message began.

The proof of what we tell you rests in your own good understanding of our wonderful truth. The basis of all that we present is in the truth that God has the substance, which He freely gives to anyone who wants it and which is the basic ingredient that impels the material result. The substance of which we speak has no element of material explanation. Therefore, we can give no material comparison.

The substance of God requires only your belief in its existence—a quite simple requirement that is set up by law. The law we speak of is inflexible because it generates what is known as optimum energy. People often use such energy once or twice in their lifetimes, but they consider the results a miracle, perhaps, or even a fluke. Perhaps if they realized it is a LAW, they would use it regularly. There are no restrictions based on religious practices. The law exists for all. Remember, the law is **that to use the vital substance of God to create what you want or desire, you must have a belief in that substance.**

Ready to move on? If not, return to the tender presences and ask for further explanation. We will wait.

When you have absorbed all that has been told above, you are ready to perform a demonstration. Team up with us here. Team up with those who require your open mind to enervate you into performing.

I checked my dictionary on the meaning of "enervate." Could these specialists mean they would deprive me of force or vigor in order that I might perform?

The meaning of the word is to weaken the being in the sense of the physical self, not the spiritual self. Yes, we want to weaken your physical response to the use of the substance that is the basis of all creative work. You must forego the use of physical means to get the teamwork required to make a physical demonstration.

I announced to my communicator that the instructions appeared to be in conflict.

No. Review, with your tender presences, the worth of their explanations to you. They never told you to put forth any physical effort, did they? No! They did not say to expect to get what you want by seeking it here or seeking it there, did they? No. The physical self must be as if asleep.

Now we proceed. The enervating of the physical self must be accomplished. If that is so, we will continue. Keep your mind open. Keep the contact with your tender presences.

Polish your imagination—the thought process by which you create a picture. The representation you must create has no eternal worth unless you put it into the inner temple of your mind where you embellish it to the best of your ability. If the imagination is not clear, and if the picture dims, you will not demonstrate.

The writer asks what she might demonstrate. The ether (God substance) is susceptible to whatever you want to enter into—securing nourishment or attaining other physical items. If you have sufficient food and shelter, you may wish to create some other good thing. Remember, the word "good" means that the thing you put into your imagination is to have the quality of God; it must not give harm to anyone, and it must be for some good purpose. A sure way to defeat this demonstration is to think in terms of acquisitiveness, for example. If there is no need for the item, no good purpose expressed, then the formation of substance into material will not take place.

Why? The whole demonstration rests on the law, remember. Review the law.

I reread the law, and I did not see anything about selfishness. Immediately, the communicator reminded me that the law reads that substance is of God.

What is God? *I was asked.* There we go back to your concept of God! Review the God concept in an earlier chapter. When you say "God," you say the word that represents your concept of all that is good, perfect and powerful. God is that essence of perfection which is there to be used. But if you perceive a God of vengeance, or a God who wants power over others, you retreat from the position of being able to use God's gifts.

The reader may find the writer's questioning helpful, though the questions may not be exactly what the reader would ask. If the reader has other questions, then he should turn to the tender presences who stand ready to help with the required answers.

Polish the picture of what you want. Bring it into the open. If it can be embellished, do so. If it needs more parts, add those. Go over it detail by detail. Now invite the tender presences to look at it. They will comment or generate a feeling about this picture. If they think you have done well, rest assured you are ready to demonstrate.

The Teammate whose Being generates your picture into materiality now takes hold. This Being, this Teammate, this God of the Universe, gives from His deep tenderness to honor your request. Team up with expectation, with the knowingness of one whose certainty is beyond question. Thank the Teammate of whom you now expect demonstration. Remove any question, any wondering. Perform.

Now we proceed to what is inevitably the most contentious of all the laws. We say "contentious" because those in the earth plane who work with this law understand its meaning, but they have very little willingness to accept it.

The law reads, **Eternalizations which you form in your mind must have your emotions weeded out.** Thoughts of real benefit to your being must not be emotional. Eternalizing truth is mental, mind over matter—not emotional. Therefore, to be successful in any demonstration, you must not generate your emotions. Put every thought of being delighted and happy or of overflowing with emotion away from you.

Surprised, I asked why emotion is detrimental to demonstration.

Because they drain energy that a person needs to make the demonstration enter into material form. The emotional tenor of each person is made up of the mind which vibrates according to how the emotion affects the individual. But this vibration is opposed to the energy vibration needed to produce the practical demonstration.

I wanted to accept this explanation, but something else intruded itself. "You said that God brought about the actual demonstration. Therefore, how could my emotions affect demonstration one way or another?" I waited, and then came the explanation.

Your being is one with the God of the Universe, one with his perfection, one with his purposes. When you eternalize, do it calmly and without undue fervor because you have no need to beg or plead your case, right? True demonstration is the product of your mind attuned to God-mind with both in teamed-up vibration. When you alter your vibration, you are altering the God concept you hold, and then you weaken the possibility of God truth pouring into the physical plane called earth.

Therefore, we say to you who intend to demonstrate, put your emotions aside in the matter of materializing the thought form which you want or need. New growth is needed within you to understand this truth, this law.

Now we move forward. Whether or not you are ready, we do not know. If you need to consider this last part, take time to do so. Thoughts from your tender presences may be called for again. Then, when you believe you are ready, read on.

The next law that we want to bring to your attention is this. **Eternal truth will be the base for your demonstration**. Here is how it works. The entity who wants to demonstrate must eternalize God's goodness, gentleness, perfection, purity and His giving of Himself and His gifts. The eternal truth in what we write here will put you in line to use what God offers. But, if you do not eternalize this eternal truth, you weaken the potential you have for making use of forthcoming teamwork.

Work for a while with what we have written here. The God truth that prevails in the use of all His gifts rests on your understanding and perfect acceptance of eternal truth. Will you attend to this matter now by going into the inner temple of your being? Will you, along with your tender presences, team up with eternal truth to your very core?

I asked this advanced spirit if my emotions will interfere when I team up with eternal truth, and here is the answer.

Emotions that cry out when you work with truth and give yourself to it wholeheartedly, will not interfere in the perfect teamwork. However, the emotional tone of your being will give you no support when you begin to demonstrate. Emotions cannot always be shut down; the mind operates first in the objective, and this is the way your own being flourishes. Emotions provide the echo. But you must master emotions. The point to this discussion is that your emotions can be a wedge that holds the creative flow in check. Your lifetime experience must tell you this.

The stronger your emotion, the weaker your entire God self. Examples of strong emotions are anger, hate, disappointment, grief, temper let loose, and the accumulation of little emotions that dominate and disturb your peace of mind. These emotions will thwart your progress in spirit for as long as they dominate you. They will make you surrender your greatest dreams and ambitions, and they try to weaken your resolve. But you, when you understand how to overcome this weakening influence, can become a strong mind at work.

The message we want to make clear in the matter of demonstration is this. Those who wring their emotions out into the waste can will take command of their lives. But those who offer their emotions as a gauge and a guide for the living of their lives may be reduced to having no lifetime experience worth mentioning. A lifetime can be wasted, it can be fruitless, and it can be the victim of unstable emotions that blow hot and blow cold.

Now eternalize this chapter's laws. Put them within your being. When you have done this work objectively and have even erased any protest to these laws, you will be ready to move forward.

Truth Requires Action

7

How can I keep my God-mind truth active and make it a powerful force in my life?

The truth of Spirit holds this planet together, keeps it stable and brings it nourishment. Truth also pours forth to be used by everyone who turns his mind to the God of the Universe. But if this truth is ignored, if it is passed by instead of being used, it is as if asleep. Then the earth receives no benefits nor does the individual.

The wisdom that comes to you, the reader, through the God-mind connection of this writer will cause you consternation, perhaps. But there is no intent to frighten you or to bring you worry. The intent here is to enlist your powerful thought waves to help in the re-creation of this planet earth.

Enter into your deepest thought concentration. Enter into the place where you become open and receptive to what God-mind presents. The teamwork that you will find there, the tender presences plus your own being, will now work together to understand this difficult chapter.

Enter herein with your mind wide awake, but with your physical self at ease. New demands place us in need of permanent truth that will not fail us at the moment of need. Therefore, you must, if you want to be among those who enter the New Age like shepherds, present an open mind at the door of universal wisdom.

Universal wisdom eternalizes within you, perhaps, as that God-like quality that is mystical or even occult. But nothing is further from the truth of the matter. There is nothing hidden here. There is nothing kept from the human being who wants the truth.

What do you think of when you think of eternal truth? What do you expect when we say you can have this truth? Everything you have known about God, everything you have eternalized as truth must be reexamined. This review means you must take this positive opportunity to focus your mind and to ignite your fervor to become one with the God of the Universe. Be a person who is open to newness of thought, not one who conforms to what has already been.

Here is how to proceed. First, put the winging truth that you receive through God-mind at the very core of your life. Then you will not be easily distracted by what "they" say, what the world expects or anything else that comes through earth-mind. Oneness with truth that comes through God-mind is indeed the first step in turning yourself over to God truth in expression.

The second step is to provide yourself with a text that you can use to eternalize all that truth can be in your life. These texts are available everywhere. They open your mind to new thoughts about your possible perfection and the reality of your being who lives forever. The text you read now is one such text, though there are others. The being you truly are, the spirit which is your reality, will be drawn to those texts that will open you to greater and greater understanding of what is indeed the best truth possible.

The third step is, of course, to give your being over to teamwork with the tender presences who will help you make a permanent God-mind connection. They will give you help to become what your being truly wants to be— one with God.

The fourth step concerns your teamwork with the God

of the Universe Who is ready to work with you in the demonstration of your truth. The truth that eternalizes within you is that which you can learn to demonstrate. When you reach this point in your growth, you will be entirely tuned to the truth eternal.

There is more. This book has thus far taken you through the first four steps, but now we enter a fifth step in your growth. Enter into this step if you think you are ready. Enter it if you believe you now possess the basic understanding of the first four steps.

Ready?

Before this chapter's transmission began, I received a preview of what was to come. The messenger told me that whether I could understand the material or not, I was to go forward. This suggestion came because I often stop when the material becomes mind boggling, and I try to deal with it by asking questions and studying the answers. This time, however, I was to still my thoughts, get out of the way, so to speak, and let the material flow.

The truth that this writer gives may propel you toward the best that you know, for she, too, opens her mind, stretches it far out and waits with expectation. New entities team up now to provide this part of the book. They come to speak through this writer who puts their words onto the word processor and thus onto paper.

These advanced spirits come to give the planet earth its opportunity to become what it may become in the way of God potential. They stride now toward this planet to be those who provide a great opportunity to each reader to enter into the work of the New Age.

The messengers settled themselves in the manner of those who enter into this teamwork, and the message proceeded.

The next step in the development of this chapter concerns your opportunity to be part of the creative process in the New Age. The eternal truth you need enters you into a giant leap of gentle understanding. We say "gentle" because those who will help you with this matter always operate with gentleness. They will help each of you to thrust aside your own particular untruths, your own particular erroneous ideas. They will reach deep within your being to the pure knowingness of you to help you to grow.

Ways that you know nothing of are now presented to enable you to become part of the creative process of the New Age. You will be able to present your own eternalizations as to what this age will accomplish. In this manner you will become a co-creator with the God of the Universe.

You who want to be part of this co-creation will accept one of the ways being readied for you. You who are keenly interested in helping to form the new earth will take this opportunity, but others may hesitate. The ways are varied, and they present a vast energy that you can tap. Therefore, never wonder how you, in and of yourself, can do this thing.

Enter into this presentation. You who want to help form the new earth will be assigned to specific tasks, and you will help those in the next plane who will work with you. The energy available to you, and to those here who team up with you, will be used for the present endeavor, and it will be of the quality which will accomplish its goal, whatever that is.

You who want to participate enter into the responsibility as well as the pleasure of working out the eternalization of what the new earth needs to be. You may want to work with certain plants to have a food base in the new earth. Or, you may join the team that wants to put new energy sources upon the new earth. Then again, you might want to help those who wrest the good which opens from God and implant it everywhere in all people. This implantation is indeed possible if you put your thought energy into the matter. The new earth can be peaceful, and you may want to help with this project.

Other assignments include the development of a pure atmosphere. Those who want to work with this assignment may do so. The purity of the atmosphere is possible if you use the energy available to you. Or, you may want to help determine what the earth will look like. What mountains would be left as they are? What mountains need new energy applied? What land will give people a place for habitation, for growing food and a place for republics to form and enter into new teamwork. Where will these places be?

Those of you who want to take part in this New Age may now get your assignments through the tender presences who will convey the matter to your mind. Then they will show you how to work, how to join perfectly with others, and how to use the energy available to create what you want.

There may be some of you who want to work with us in the matter of bringing the truth of God into the race of people who inhabit the earth. The truth will stabilize them, give them a base for their lives, for their work, for their planning. This work can be yours, too, if you want.

As you read these words, new thoughts penetrate into the teamwork. The ideas seem strange to many, but they are exciting to others. We say to those who enter with excited optimism, YOU are the one we want to take one of these assignments. You may have thought of another area you want to participate in. That is fine. Tell the tender presences who work with you. They will help you to work in this way.

Gentleness pervades this work, gentleness that is both energetic and teamed up with whatever is the good of the universe. Eternal wisdom is ready to be opened to you if you but step through the door. Take the step by turning your thoughts toward the helping spirits, and you will enter into the most exciting endeavor ever offered to beings of earth.

You have been given an opportunity to participate in this new creation. If you wet the entire idea down with earth-mind thoughts, you simply lose the way to adventure. The New Age is just that, you know, adventure. But if you bring your own experience to it, your own willingness to work, you will team up with the New Age with nothing less than great enthusiasm.

Now go to those who work with you to let them know

your questions or your choice of work, if you are ready to make it. Team up with all that is possible to bring about in this new earth, and you will lead the way into everything that mankind wants.

The interesting part of the creativity of the new earth is that you will participate in the project yourself. That way you will not consider yourself merely a victim of circumstances when the New Age comes, but rather, you will become a part of the project.

Now some of you may want nothing to do with this because you see no good coming about in the change the earth will make. But some of you will evaluate the whole thing and find you have an opportunity here to fashion the kind of earth you want.

The entering truth is resumed by the communicator who first began this chapter. This one now enters to provide you with needed background in this matter of truth.

Without skipping a beat, the former communicator continued.

Before mankind ever began to have form, the truth of the universe was within the earth. You may marvel at these words, for you may suppose that truth only enters the mind of mankind. The earth, however, is an organism in its own way. Let me explain.

The earth was formed by those who wanted to put their truth to work in the universe. Those who put their understanding into project earth interred good elements within it, elements that were basically made up of the one substance called "truth." Those who worked their universal truth into the form that you now enjoy placed their beings into the very crust of the earth. How? By entering into that which was good and pure and beautiful. Then they stayed there to help it continue its creativity. Thus they became one with the planet.

In that way, the whole process developed with the eternalizations of truth generated by those creative spirits. They wrested all that was good into the plan; they sent away that which did not give good to the planet. These who did this work eternalized what was fair, what

56

was pure and what was of eternal worth. That way the earth itself is an entity, for it is held together by those who create, those who put themselves at the core of the earth's teamwork.

The creative spirit of planet earth now judges the planet's handiwork (the changes people have brought about upon the earth) beside that which eternal truth brought into being. With consummate care, those who bring their creative energy into play now eternalize new growth, new purifying and new goodness. But those who do this work need the new energy which is provided through the God of the Universe. Here is where you come in. You who may decide to join in the creativity will have access to this energy and will be able to use it in wonderful ways to help those who initially gave the earth that which was good. Those who began this project need strength and energy, and they need the truth interred once again.

They can do this alone, of course. But when they work alone, they must work with only the earth itself in mind, not mankind. Those of you now in the earth plane, however, will have mankind in mind as you give your own strength, your own expertise, your own gentleness into the new creative plan. That way the New Age will arrive with greater gentleness than if you simply leave it up to those creative intelligences who have entrusted the earth with its truth that now needs replenishing.

The truth that was interred here has been wrested from its moorings. The truth that has held the earth in its orbit and provided its good has been destabilized by those who heed only the earth-mind truth of the Users. Those who go forth to use, to take from the earth without replenishing, have robbed the earth of its basic strength. The initial truth that developed a good earth was demonstrated in the beauty and magnificent goodness which emanated from universal wisdom.

Therefore, those of you who earnestly want to help, who desire to make the transition into the New Age helpful to mankind instead of a jarring action, may help bring about an easier method. Here is your opportunity, your truth that can be worked into creative endeavors. Therefore, the choice is yours—the harsh method that nearly begins the earth process again or the gentle process which herds people like sheep into the safer places where they may bring forth abundance. Those who survive the change into the New Age will have their method of survival provided for them if you who understand what is being said will take this opportunity to help.

Those who have lived upon this planet for the ages of man include both you, the reader, and I the spirit who brings you this message. We all went to the earth time and time again to enter into a life form to eternalize our growth plan. Those who determine to live according to their growth plan do not harm the earth. Rather, they bring forth fruit, bring forth good, and they also replenish. But those who fail to enact their growth plan only take from the earth and leave very little of value behind. They try again and again, of course, but the earth has suffered through the many ages of man.

The truth that was put into the earth eternalized all that mankind would ever need or want if those needs and wants were generous in their thought and not selfish. Again, the Users versus the Givers. Those who brought pain to life put the truth into a deep sleep of non-productive value. Why? Because truth only prospers when it is used again and again. Use proliferates truth, not vice versa. There is no way to explain such a thing in earth-mind language, for earth truth insists on the idea that there is only so much of anything.

The truth gradually depleted itself because it was not used. That is why we come now to this New Age. The truth that sleeps gives no powerful energy, you see. It is there, yes. But only those who created the earth have been loyal to it. Now those creative entities know no other way than to enter the earth into a great stirring up, a heaving and awful wrenching that will eternalize new truth that is active and which has force. But what a hard time for those who live upon its face! Therefore, you have the opportunity to perform this creative task, this beautiful way of giving new heart to an old and miserable entity—planet earth.

Now give us your best thought projection. We mean by this to project your thought about this earth into the thought form which can be made true. The earth, a big and lovely sphere, has a ring of mold around it now. Enter into a new picture of the gentle breath of the God of the Universe—the pure optimum eternalization of purity that surrounds the earth. There it is! Open your mind to it. The crystal clear teamwork that provides what this earth needs immediately in its outer atmosphere—the ring of purity! Hold it in mind. Project it outward. Then project it downward as you see this planet from above. Together we make this creative thrust.

Put the energy out there where it can operate. The entering truth will stem the tide of things and help us hold the planet together while we—you and we and those who began this earth project—work in tandem to bring the New Age into being.

The chapter comes to a close, and you have the opportunity to evaluate things as we have presented them. Then we will give you the energy, the power, the eternalizations that will make a difference in this planet you call home.

How to Communicate Spirit to Spirit

8

Why is the actual communication with God-mind and the Brotherhood necessary if my life is to develop to its potential?

Team up with those who can help you to perfect your communication skills. This chapter is written to give you the truth about this manner of communication—spirit to spirit—and to present our good thoughts on the subject. The way to get your being on target as far as teaming up with the tender presences and the God-mind connection is to be concerned enough to read our suggestions and then try them on your own. Practice is the precious key to success, and without this key, communication is not possible.

Without this spirit to spirit exchange, nothing of eternal worth happens in your life. Without this communication, you dangle openly at the end of the eternal truth, hoping, but not getting to the upward goal. The eternal truth is not hard to get, you know, but it must team up with you in some way or other. That is why we who enter your plane to help will stand ready to help you make this connection.

Be a total communicator, not a person who only thinks about the God-mind connection, a person who stands there immobilized and impotent. Those who do not make this connection send their thoughts heavenward, looking to God as the Man in the Sky. They either fear this God concept of their own making, or they simply cannot make themselves believe that God is there in the personal.

We have already brought you material about working with the total potential of God, about putting your concept of God into an open-ended belief that will allow it to expand and expand. Remember, we want to help you, or we would not chastise those who still think about God in a primitive way.

Better communication is possible if you will open your mind to the possibility. The reality is spirit, remember. You, we, God—we are all spirit. Therefore, our communication is entered into with this understanding. The earth body part of you is not the teammate we speak to. The one we talk to here is your reality, your spirit self. Your body is your vehicle of expression in the earth plane. Therefore, know that though you operate on that plane as one entity, it is your mind who rules, not your physical self.

Put the thought behind you that your body has anything at all to do with our communication. We here in this next plane of life have no material bodies that we can show you in the earth plane. The bodies we have are real enough, but they do not constitute what is material in earth understanding. This fact does not limit us! It frees us to be better helpers who can respond to your call.

To communicate, put the thought in your mind that we can do this thing because we speak spirit to spirit. There is NOTHING eerie or strange in this communication. There is NOTHING of what some call witchcraft! Who believes in witches, anyway? Our communication is straightforward. It is possible because we were meant in the beginning to have this contact with God-mind.

The writer thinks there might be an explanation due here about the term "God-mind." When we use that term, we refer to the aspect of God that we call "Mind." God is many sided, many faceted. He is Principle, Law, Energy, Tenderness, Wholeness, the Truth of the Universal Presence. He is Mind. And when we speak of a God-mind connection, we speak of touching that Mind communicatively. Why can this be done? Because you, we, all spirit entities, enter into oneness with the God from whom we took our life, our being, our hope for reunion.

In the beginning, we were meant to enter earth life and retain this God-mind connection which we would use to improve the earth, to help us to live up to our growth patterns. Those of you who have read the first trilogy* know about growth patterns, but let us review them briefly here.

Growth patterns are those individual plans we make before we plunge back into earth life again. These patterns give us the way by which we can become improved spirits who gain the godly attributes. A growth pattern is made after we have lived a lifetime experience and have, in this plane, reexamined it as well as previous lifetimes. When we have analyzed the whole, we may still need to return to earth life to complete our growth. If so, we make a growth pattern for our next lifetime, and it is that which we intend to enact when we once again enter life.

But entering as we do in infant form, we struggle into maturity not quite aware of the spirit who wants to enact its plan. The way it was meant to be, however, was that each could communicate with God-mind and learn the plan and gain wisdom in how to enact it in the lifetime experience in which we find ourselves.

But mankind entered into the darkness of total oblivion of the nature of God. Instead of connecting with God-mind, people filled themselves with the truth that they told one another. What progress could be made when God-mind communication stopped? Advanced spirits came to earth to reunite man and God. Some were well received, and some were not. Those who were well received became the saints or leaders whom people tried to

---

*The Trilogy of Truth, by Jean K. Foster: The God-Mind Connection, 1987. The Truth that Goes Unclaimed, 1987. Eternal Gold, 1988. Kansas City, Uni*Sun.

worship, but not imitate. The communication these advanced ones taught became (in the minds of mankind) the proof of their greatness, not the proof that all mankind can communicate.

Yes, mankind still stands aloof from the possibility of their oneness with the truth that pours in volumes these days telling them to turn to God who will tell them the truth of their beings. Many turn to churches—to men and women who know only church dogma—to find their own answers. How could a church give you what you in your own particular circumstances need to grow? How could those who wear robes and who hold formal services reach into your own spirit with the advice and counsel your own soul needs?

No, whether the pulpit is filled with those in robes or those who wear the regular garb of men—or women—the congregation is only told the version of truth that one person presents at that moment. What irresponsible opinion! You—we—need absolute truth. Yes, "absolute." This truth is not given from God to one or two in the earth plane. The marvel is, if you think of it as a marvel, that ONE AND ALL CAN RECEIVE GOD TRUTH!

The Perfection, the Power, the Tenderness, the Energy, the Truth Magnificent—this is the God we speak of here. It is this God to whom you can go to open lines of communication. We here in this next plane of life are the helpers, the advanced spirits who enter your life experience only when you want us. We, however, can help you open these lines of communication. Therefore, why wait?

What is communication with God? It is a two-way thought transference between you and that Mind. You know that you think thoughts, right? That they may be received by another is proved in laboratories, so we need not discuss that kind of communication here. Therefore, thought communication is not only a possibility in your mind; it is proved there in the earth plane. What hinders your belief in what we speak? What keeps those of you who wait from entering into this God-mind connection?

There have been many throughout the ages who have

entered into this communication. They may not express it in the way we do, but they may indicate it in some other way. Some say "inspiration" came to them. Others say "they had a strange dream." The energy of thought pursues us and teams up with us in the universal ether. People have a hard time denying it. Given the true understanding of the matter, what now deters you from acting?

The noblest spirits known to man have been great communicators with God-mind. We could name them, but why? The point is that you must understand that this communication is not saved for the "great." It is there for YOU. Now we must proceed with the way to improve communication if you have already begun this, or if you have not yet begun, we will point out ways to begin now.

Good thoughts produce good in your world. This truth is espoused by churches. Though churches tend to herd people through one narrow door of thought, they still send out some truth. Be your own being, not one who is herded, not one who tries only what the church approves! Why, if mankind waited for church approval before moving ahead spiritually, the earth would still be in the dark ages!

Those who espouse God from the pulpits tend to denounce man at the same time. Why? We—you in the earth plane and we in this next plane of life—began as offshoots of God. Why denounce the spirit who entered life as part of God's plan?

Team up with the idea that you have been trusted with a great responsibility. Yes, that responsibility is to live in an earth body that enables you to enact your growth plan. This plan brings you into the universal plan that allows all spirits to advance step by step throughout many lifetimes. The church threw out this wisdom when it organized under the Christian banner, when it found the belief in reincarnation too enervating to many. Yes, many people simply did not try to enact the growth plan because they knew they had another chance at life. So, the church leaders threw out the belief, refused to teach it ever again, and in its place they brought in the damnation of souls as the tool by which people could be forced into the goodness of God!

The wisdom of the church brought about beliefs in purgatory, for example. Those who now call themselves "Bible churches," think they know it all because they know what their version of the Bible says. Were they there when the Bible was first written? Teaming up with one source of truth, the Bible, they invent all the rest of their religious ways. They fret over minute matters. They wrest the evil of the world out into the open and parade it around that all may see it. What good is this? How does this ascertainment of what is without goodness result in mankind making individual contact with God? We in this Brotherhood wince and tenderly give preachers our thoughts when they enter into tirades against whatever they want eradicated.

Poor benighted people who turn to evil as the subjects of their sermons! Those who listen promote fear in their own hearts and judgment against others. How does this bring them into contact with God? They are too busy pointing their fingers at others to see the great void in their own lives! They are too eternally prone to be workers in the church organization and not workers in their Father God's vineyard!

Beware of those who lead you with their fury or with their own wisdom, for they do not come to you from God! They come to you only on their own behalf. Those who speak to congregations enter into great responsibility, for they set themselves up as the shepherds who would bring you closer to God. What foolishness! The only one who can bring you closer to God is YOU.

This writer finds this part hard to write, but she keeps at it. We realize that she does not like the controversial aspects of this book, but she wants to be true to the message we bring. There may be some who condemn these words. In fact, there will be many who condemn them. However, the words you read here are mild compared to the truth in this matter. The writer would indeed have trouble bringing you the message that we often think should be presented!

The object, we think, in a church organization should be to help you to connect with God in your way. There are some preachers, priests, rabbis, leaders of denominations and the so-called truth preservers all around the world who think it their duty to hold to the truth as their particular group identifies it. Never mind what God-mind says! They adhere to their own truth without change. The progress which these groups make is nil. They bind themselves with the chains of their past, the ropes of their present, and they cement it all in place with energy that runs to great abandon!

But to put it all in perspective, let us turn now to the communication that is there for all. Even within the churches they speak of this communication. But if that communication leads you into any direction they do not understand, they condemn it as from the non-existent devil. But God speaks through God-mind to each of you according to the understanding of your particular spirit. Those in the next plane of life, the Brotherhood of God, will help each person with this connection. The Brotherhood are the Counselor, the Comforter, the Holy Spirit (communicator) promised by Jesus to his followers.

No, the Brotherhood of God is not Christian in the definition of churches. We are, however, those who have turned our lights to the One Great Light which is God. The one who made the perfect demonstration, Jesus, brings his own words to you on this matter.

MY MESSAGE OF HOPE
FROM JESUS

The truth that can enter your own spirit/mind is within the One whom we call God. This Greatness is our one Center, our One Understanding. To rid yourselves of unnecessary fears or to rid yourselves of disbelief, turn the eternal truth over to your own spirit mind. What response is there? When I speak to you of the Greatness which is God, do you want this Greatness in your life? When I speak of the Tenderness which is God, do you want that Tenderness in your life? When I speak of the Perfection or the Wholeness or the Prosperity of God, do you want these things? The spirit within you does indeed cry out for each quality.

What needs do you have? What desires do you hold dear? What goals are set for your life? What 'unanswerable' questions stir in your heart? These can all be met with responses from God-mind, responses that will transform your life and bring you into oneness with all that Is, with All that Exists as Good. Here is your answer, then. It is your innate character that cries out for contact with the God of the Universe.

Jesus' message ended, and the messenger from the Brotherhood continued.

The way to communicate with those who are there to help you is simply to team up with the belief that they are there. Without this belief factor, there is a problem of activating your extrasensory mechanism. The working of this communication, though not difficult from our standpoint here in this next plane of life, is not without problems from your viewpoint. The physical being is persistent in its wavering attitudes toward that which is not visible to the earth eye. But you, with your mind open, may be the great control factor in this communication.

This control factor, your mind, must take charge. It means that your spirit rules your body without equivocation. This determination results in expanded consciousness and the energy needed to be in the open channel that takes your mind and connects it with God-mind. The tender presences will help you with this. They are advanced spirits who understand your earth/spirit approach to communication. It is they who know how you, a unique entity who has certain ways of gaining understanding, will be able to enter into communication easily. Therefore, let them help.

Here is one example that may help you. One entity believed in the idea that communication was possible to this plane of life. She wrote her belief in her heart of hearts, and she pursued the idea even during the physical body's sleep. This person gained understanding and we managed to touch base with her conscious mind in relation to her destiny.

She opened herself fully to communication, knowing its possibilities, believing in her potential, and she gained the ability to communicate with ease. She not only communicates with her tender presences, but she communicates with those who have left the earth plane and now rest in this second plane of life. She teams up with whomever she wishes to in order to continue her great interest in those no longer visible in the earth plane. This one now enters into great projects that the tender presences awakened her to, and finally she learned to get into the open channel without their help. Gently she learns through God-mind how to live her life, how to deal with difficult situations, how to gain and hold mastery over herself.

What she has done is possible for all. You, reader, may gain insight into your life in the earth plane, and you may gain new understanding, new truth, new eternalizations to make your lifetime experience joyful. These are the possibilities with communication.

Each person is indeed different. Different in body, yes, but also different in spirit. Each has a potential unlike that of any other. Therefore, you need never feel you are trapped within the framework of your life. You need never feel that life holds you by the throat. You, the one-with-God person who can soar with eagles, need not reduce your life to making earth compromises that will only lead to disappointment.

Team up with your potential by turning to us who wait to help you to communicate with ease. The entity who writes this book opens her mind to this plane with such certainty that it is as if she is here. This writer does not see us—no, she has not learned that. She does not hear us either, but she is in communication thought to thought. It is the way we speak together here in this plane of life—thought to thought. There is no deception, no way to prove yourself because your every thought opens to us.

Therefore, at this point, we tell you to decide, to believe in the possibility, to open your mind to our presence. With this teamwork, we will help you to make your God-mind connection. To get the details of this subject, return to the first trilogy* which answers the question of how to communicate.

The truth that propels you toward this wonderful communication enters through the open channel. This channel is the connection between your mind and the mind of God. The way to get this connection is to put your being into readiness by stilling the body, turning to the God self within and putting your teamwork into the hands of the tender presences. With this contact established, you know you are in good hands.

The writer wants us to discuss the teamwork of communication to a greater degree. The writer realizes that some may enter into this communication for purposes other than entering into God-mind truth. There may be some who want to communicate because they are curious, for example. Others may want to provide themselves with an interesting cloak of better wisdom— apparent to others, but not really solid. Your reason for entering into communication is important, of course.

Why would you want the help, advice and counsel of the tender presences? We hope it is because you earnestly want to learn the perfect truth for your own soul, to be one with God-mind that will tell you exactly

---

*The Trilogy of Truth, by Jean K. Foster: The God-Mind Connection, 1987. The Truth that Goes Unclaimed, 1987. Eternal Gold, 1988. Kansas City, Uni*Sun.

what you need and want to know. But if your motives center around a desire for greater approval from others or for personal elevation to a lofty position, you are definitely on the wrong track.

There are those in this next plane of life who still adhere to earth truth. They enter into nothing of value here and merely wait until they can leap back into life again. They learn nothing, they make no plan for another lifetime, and they wrest their only pleasure through susceptible earth plane entities who look to someone "on this side" to tell them what they hope to hear.

And what do such entities hope to hear? They turn to whoever responds and wait for words that reflect their own motives in communicating. They often fall prey to those on this side who delight in controlling an earth entity. But such things never happen if you truly want God-mind truth. Those who would control you know nothing of God-mind and they fall away, unable to get in touch with you.

In this plane the spirits who cluster together have similar beliefs, tones, reasons for their actions. When you enter into communication without the godly teamwork, you leave yourself open to a cluster of spirits who reject God truth. Therefore, when you hear of someone who communicated with those on the next plane and you hear negative things about that communication, you can count on it that there were, initially, thoughts of eternal **opinion** that has nothing to do with God truth.

Contact with God-mind enters with gentle thoughts. Never does God-mind jolt or jar you. Never does God-mind truth bring you orders. The God of the Universe treads softly and teams up only when you open yourself to His teamwork. To team up with anything less than God is to enter into thinking that reflects your own weakness. Therefore, if you team up with weakness, expect to be controlled, ordered about and given truth that is questionable, to say the least.

Know, reader, that God-mind truth enters with a tender even flow. The being who you are will never refuse God truth because it will team up with your being to bring help, goodness and perfection. Therefore, if you feel you must somehow test the truth you receive, you now know how. The God of the Universe knows you live in the earth plane, and He intends to help you to unfold your truth in a practical manner there where you live. There is no truth given that is not directed at the unfolding of your growth plan.

If there is anything to question, do so. If there is anything to doubt, be a doubter. The tender presences stand ready to answer questions, turn you to God-mind truth and to change erroneous thoughts into those that are error free. There is nothing to fear if you will remember these gentle ones who help you.

Therefore, enter into communication to make your life fill with power and joy. Enter into communication in order to be a person who puts truth into expression. Team up with the tender presences, and team up with the God of the Universe. Here is our message, our right thought, our best presentation.

The Turnabout

9

What is this TRUTH that we can use to create whatever is needed or desired?

Those who wish to survive the New Age with optimum mastery over their conditions need to be turnabouts who rely only on God truth. Those who turn themselves to the discovery of God truth, the wisdom that pours in to open minds, will find that they meet any problem that presents itself. This claim is not too great, reader, for you need only basic understandingif you are to accomplish your potential.

Regard the matter we lay before you in the light of cool judgment. Team up with us to review the facts of the New Age situation. Those who rely on the wisdom of God will go forward with eternal truth enacted in their individual lives. They will team up with those from this plane who can help them, and they will open themselves to the truth that will give them their necessities. This kind of truth will never be stolen, nor will it be lost. It will penetrate to your heart and remain there.

With this Pure Truth within you, you will go about the living of your life without fear of being robbed of your valuables, for your valuables are within. Those who take whatever they want—the food and water supplies, housing—will find that they have displaced you only momentarily, for you will reproduce all that you had before.

What kind of truth will do such things? Why, the truth that pours out to you from God-mind and rises from within the Greatness which we call God—the Source that never runs dry.

The Source of All never runs dry nor does it deplete. You will understand this wisdom as you grow. Teaming up with the tender presences will help you with the understanding and then with the growth. The tender presences unite with you to bring you into the New Age that now impends. The wisdom teams up with all that needs to be done—the co-creative work, the inner preparation and the realization of what you will need.

Now put your own being, your reality or mind, into our gentle hands. Your reality yearns to be free of everything that will result in disappointment in the New Age. By putting your reliance upon what is material, you will suffer the turmoil that will inevitably come. But by filling your inner being with wisdom and understanding, you will no doubt stride forth with confidence.

The New Age is frightening to many because they consider the totality of change. The best way to approach this growth period is to put the wisdom of God within so you will have no room for fear. Those who react will have terrible agonies, but those who prepare themselves will rush forward with enthusiasm to enact their truth.

How can this be? How can the human being which you are ever get to the point when he or she depends on the inner self and its guidance from those in the next plane? Why, it is not as novel as you might think! There are people who today have God truth within them, people who meet their days with the knowledge of their own truth enacted in their lives.

You would no doubt like to meet these people, but they are private persons, unable to stand on pedestals or to team up with the media who might take notice of their wisdom. These whom we tell you of offer themselves in quiet ways. They do not seek to impress or to spend their days in political arenas. They enter daily into the wisdom which pours in to them, and they work with this wisdom within their beings where they learn how to use it in practical ways.

Now is the time when we call for the turnabout—one who enters into the idea but who does not quite understand how to be what we describe. You, many of you anyway, open your minds to wisdom, but you fail to go the second mile into successful use of the wisdom. Perhaps you only consider this wisdom something to talk about. It is nice to be able to discuss such things with others. But to give it a permanent place in your life? To give it the energy that takes it into day by day living? Most simply retreat from this position.

Turn yourselves about! Turn to the tender presences, the God-mind truth, the opportunity to ·enter the New Age standing squarely on your feet without fear! That is what this chapter is about—the call to be a turnabout.

Make no judgment yet about what we have brought to you, for we have another side of the picture to present. Those who now rely on the energy of earth-mind, those who empty their universal wisdom upon the trash heap in favor of what is now seen or heard or touched with their human body will know no peace when the New Age comes. Why? Here is the reason.

The temple which was raised will now be brought down! This statement, which you may have read, is true today. The temples of earth (truth)—buildings, powerful machines, ever expanding technology, earth's resources as they are now known—all will tumble into the inner being of the earth. The tumbling will reduce it all into the elements from which matter came and will thus restore (God) truth into the earth.

How will you or any animal or plant form survive? We speak to you now to tell you there will be an opportunity to escape and endure. There are some of you who read this and say you don't want to survive. Then you will not. But there are others who know they are destined to survive. They feel this call within them. They enter into the opportunity, but they wonder how they can withstand such turmoil.

We tell you over and over, but perhaps even yet you do not understand. The eternal truth which is of God is your greatest asset! This truth will place you in the teamwork that will prepare you to survive. You will know where you can go to be safe and learn how you will live, how you will eat and how you will find shelter. There you will begin the greatest opportunity you can imagine.

Still some of you shake your heads! "What is this *truth*?" they say, "that it can provide me food and shelter?" *Truth*, my friend, is not the open philosophical thought that wafts here and there without roots! *Truth* is the only everlasting reality within this universe or in any other universe. *Truth* is the highest technological essence that the universe provides. No one in the earth plane has even conceived of such advancement as is possible within *truth*. No, I realize you cannot totally grasp what we give you here, but yet you must try anyway.

Put your visualization factor into play here. The *truth* that we try to teach you about is opening itself to you. Sit at a table together, you and the tender presences. There make the God-mind connection that releases the flow of perfect *truth*.

We get together to give you powerful energy that enters by means of the eternalizations that you and the presences work through. The *truth* from God-mind is the focus of our attention, and it moves toward you in its perfection.

Enter into a visualization that we now present. *Truth* is the focus. Yet, somehow we must project this word into a visualization of what it truly is—*the only greatness that brings everything that is into physical being.* That is right. *Truth*, as we use it here, *is the Pure Truth which is that power, that generating influence upon matter that enters the earth plane to bring about creativity.*

The elements which scientists have discovered in the formation of matter open themselves to arrangement due to the *truth* of our present focus. Enter into a visualization here. Breathe the word "truth" gently toward the earth that is part of your own environment. Then breathe the same word again. Wait a second or two while the word sails out and penetrates the earth.

The earth stirs and dust rises. But wait! It is not really dust. What you see are the actual elements, normally too small for the regular earth eye to see, stirring themselves into activity. You breathe again, and this time you breathe, "*Truth* enters your very core and holds you in its grip. The *truth* enters God's blessing into your core and stirs you with joy. Good, purity, eternal tenderness flow into that which you are. Receive this *truth* with joy, all you elements, all you energetic particles."

In this way you enfold new *truth* into the old and worn earth which now enters its upheaval. By entering this blessing of *truth* into the elements, you help the spirit of creativity that wants to provide the earth with all that it needs.

I asked the messenger if we can specify what kind of truth we breathe into the elements—like purity or some other quality.

The messenger replied:

The *truth* that we want you to help put back into the earth is the composite goodness of the One Who Is. The *truth* is that which enters with the elements as the purity you mention plus all the eternal characteristics such as tenderness, wholeness, goodness, mercy and understanding. You who know and believe that earth is indeed an entity whose spirit is now depleted will recognize what we say as the utmost in positive action.

To be a perfect helper in the New Age project, breathe the goodness of God back into the earth. The energy with which to do this is ready to use. It is that which is freely given by the Universal Intelligence to restore one of its own. Therefore, think with positive force that you want to hold the *truth* before your face that you may breathe it back into the earth.

God breathed goodness into formation. The idea of breath is likened here to the energy that goes forth to make the connection complete. You, God's partner who teams up to help in the new creation, may use this powerful energy when you breathe *truth* back into the earth.

This message is optimistic and helpful. Once you understand you have this opportunity to be helpful, you need not cower or cringe in the cave of ignorance. You need not pour your ebbing strength into some hole or other. You can stand erect in the face of things to come because you have within you the entire teamwork that will help you to lead not only yourself and your loved ones to godly living, but will help you lead others also. Our entire focus at this point is to team up with as many of you as possible that we may work together to make the New Age the wonderful experience it can be.

Those who reject what we present in the way of opportunity literally turn their backs on the eternal truth that is God's very Self pouring into their beings. Yes, those who turn away, snicker or laugh outright will not use *truth* at all. They will depend on earth truth which will never see them safely through the upcoming New Age. These who reject the opportunity remain as they are, slaves to the energy that this tired earth puts forth. These people will cry out and want help when the time comes. They will blame everyone except themselves. They will try to take from those who have and generally cause emotional and physical turmoil.

Only the ones who practice *truth* in the way we have stated here will be saved. The words are not a threat! They are not meant to frighten you. They are merely the facts as we report them from this plane. We here can see the thought waves of earth. They rise with increasing frequency now, and they gasp with great turbulence. Earth is giving out her signals that the creative spirit that has held her together through the ages is about to relinquish its hold. When that happens, either the earth will flatten and depress, or it must go into new creative upheaval. The spirit of the earth itself prepares it now for upheaval.

But those of you who read this may enter into partnership with God's purposes and work with His energy in helping the creative force to stabilize earth's forces. Then the upheaval will not mean nearly total destruction of all that is; rather, it will mean that the renewal will, indeed, be less traumatic and will generate more tenderness in its work. This is your challenge, your opportunity.

We here join with you there in this commitment to the planet earth, and we want no one to think we do not care. There is much caring here, and we want to help you to survive—yes, but not only that. We want to help you to enter the New Age with all consummate power over the conditions you find.

Thoughts now swirl around you. They travel in the powerful twisting energy that takes you upward in understanding, upward in the wonderful truth that enters through God-mind. We promise you now that you will not be forgotten in the coming age, nor will you be left without resources. Plans now underway will reach their perfection by that time, and you will participate in that eternal greatness. These are not "just words"! No! Words are the powerful expression of thought, and thought is everything in the way of creativity.

The templing of these words with your understanding is what we want to work with next. Those who enter into the opportunity will undoubtedly want to be one with their own personal truth. Therefore, it is to these we now address ourselves.

Be unweakened in the face of the challenge before you, for to weaken now would be tantamount to resuming your partnership with earth-mind truth. This is no time to be reopening your earth-mind truth. The decision is made. The time is near. With every ounce of the best that is within you, team up with the truth that arrives to be your very own. Then hold on.

The time of the New Age approaches, and no doubt you want to know just when. The exact time is written where the God of the Universe puts these things, but the exact date is not open to us here in this plane. Those who

79

know the time now rush to reenter the entire earth plane to give their best help. Yet, there is no hint as to the exact day, the exact time.

We know what is happening, however. We see the turn of events. We hear the weakened thoughts of the earth. But eternalizations of the way we will be warned are not yet clear. We hold *truth* of God self-evident—that the earth needs replenishing, and the time is near.

Other writers have written that the turn of the century is the time. A few say sooner than that. I asked for a comment.

Those who say they know may indeed know. But we here in this plane do not have the exact time. We have the evidence before us. We team up with all the universal wisdom which points to the upheaval and renewal. Therefore, we want people to take hold of the situation now and bring to it their own creative spirit which will give the earth help.

Some books describe an upheaval and various changes on the face of the earth which people find frightening. I again asked for a comment.

Yes, change is frightening, but changes are inevitable. Those who expect to enter a new heaven on earth will be disappointed. Nothing on the face of the earth will be the same. Nothing will have the appearance that it had before. Therefore, we advise you to expect complete change. The way to team up with change is to embrace it, welcome it, get in tune with it. That is our message which we propel toward you through this writer.

The teammate who writes the book urges us to comment in some way upon the time element involved. But there is no way we can be exact. The only bearing the time factor has is to enter you into the creativity now so that you will be ready. But all who read this book will not all live to that time. Each of you must work with your tender presences to know whether you will enter that time or not. They, by the way, will keep you informed of the changes they detect in the earth.

The "when" is not important. The "where" is very important. The earth is depleted—this earth, the one you enjoy, the one we have all enjoyed. We all want to preserve this planet—you who live your present lifetimes upon it and we in this plane who have lived lifetime after lifetime there. This project we have outlined in this chapter will bring help to what we truly care about—the perfected earth. Therefore, do not become distracted with the exact day.

We do not hedge! The writer thinks we might be hedging. No! Now is the time—we do know that—to turn to *truth* for helping this earth make a change upon its axis.

The axis will shift. What has been the North Pole will no longer be. The poles will simply be located opposite one another in new areas of the earth. The shift will be tremendously unnerving unless you help with the process. Those presences who stand by to help you will explain your role in greater detail, so on that day of upheaval, you will look up from your work and say, "Oh yes! Now it begins!"

Be the turnabout who releases his hold upon earth-mind and turns now to God-mind truth.

Eternal Truth— Your Creative Power

10

What is creative power? How can I tap into it and use it to bring beauty and value into the earth plane?

Facing the New Age takes a great deal of courage, but we can develop the strength and confidence we need if we understand the truth God has for us. Truth, remember, is more than an idea, more than words on paper. "Truth is," according to the Brotherhood of God, "that which makes it possible to be in charge of your world and your own conditions."

This chapter develops an understanding of what these advanced spirits call "eternal truth." Personal truth, that which enters through the open channel our tender presences help us to develop, is for our individual spirits. Eternal truth, however, is that which pours indiscriminatingly upon us all to help us use our creative powers.

The Brotherhood continued.

No one who ever thought about the projected good that can be brought into a lifetime experience will want to miss this chapter. It is about making eternal truth your tool to help you to meet the needs of the New Age.

First, consider what eternal truth is. It is the positive thrust that God pours over all who turn their minds to Him. The eternal truth opens itself to everyone, of course, but it can only help those who understand its true function. This particular truth consists of those understandings that are universally accepted as God principles.

"Universally accepted" does not mean people vote upon the matter. It means that God principles govern the universal teamwork or better creativity. Eternal truth is never disturbed by what you or anyone else thinks of it; the truth is the truth regardless of earth opinions. The truth we speak of here is not wasted in the manner of that which you can decide to put aside—your personal truth, for example. Eternal truth operates because it must.

To use this truth to your advantage, team up with the Brotherhood who invite you to understand and then make use of eternal truth. The reason eternal truth is not able to benefit a great many people is because they team up with what opposes it, thus creating a neutral or nonproductive point. The only way to profit from these eternal God principles is not to resist them. Put yourself in the flow, and then you can rest in the truth that will enhance your own life.

Watch while we explain and outline the possibilities. Watch while we pour generous, gentle, tender growth into your being! Be entirely comforted by our tenderness and won over by our gentle manner. There is no one here who is vengeful or who will bring bad tidings. We, here, only want to enter into more teamwork, more generous giving.

Eternal truth promises to enter into everything that is creative. You who want to live creatively will benefit by teaming up with this creative principle. Think to yourself, "I want to build the kind of vehicle that will use untapped power." Then turn to the eternal truth, to that principle which promises to work on behalf of creativity. Naturally, you remember that anything of God must work toward the good of life, toward a generous act, toward that which will become the universal good.

Work in the truth which proclaims the creative spirit that wants to help you to attain your goals. Though we mentioned but one example, the creativity principle works for all kinds of creativity. What do you want to create? Is it beautiful? Is it useful? Do you want to do this creative project because of its intrinsic worth for the general good of earth and its inhabitants? Then it qualifies as that which will receive the God principle's benefits.

Rest assured that this principle works. It is based on the all-good promise of God: "The world will receive its good, and the people will bring forth good." Those of you who comprehend that this principle means that everyone may take part in the creative good, are entering into perfect understanding.

Each thought which opens itself to a physical form is eternalized through the principle of creativity that God Himself put into effect. Therefore, the God principle that we speak of here opens every good, inventive, creative thought to use in the earth plane.

Team up with the principles, and you will work seeming miracles in your life experience. The "miracles," will not be miraculous at all—just the working out of what is available in the way of proven principles.

The principle that will provide you the most help, in all probability, is that which works with the eternalizing of what you need and want in your life experience. The working out of this principle will be practical in the event that you need necessary things like sustenance and protection. **The principle is that which honors the promise by God that He is the Teammate Whom you may count on, the Teammate Who gives His help, His tender care, His fatherly gifts to His children—you.**

With this principle working through you, all your stated needs and wants can be met. Evidenced here is the truth that there is this Caring God, this Wonderful Goodness, this Best Giver of what you must have to live your life. To enact the principle, you must, of course, accept it as truth. Then you must accept it as principle. Finally, the principle of truth sends you whatever you must have to live well.

I interrupted the messenger to ask, "If I do not accept the truth as a principle which works on my behalf, but only admit intellectually that the Bible indicates that God is a Father God who gives good gifts, what will this mean for me?"

The truth stated in the Bible is, of course, eternal. But understanding it as principle is the key to having it work in your personal life. Otherwise, the truth is only the promise of God towards those in the days when the Bible was written or when the words were first given to those who listened. Then, for you, the message is simply historical, not practical.

Terminate any thought that God is historical. The truth will not help you one iota if you persist in considering what God Is from the historical point of view. God Is from the practical point of view, and that is what we, here, want to communicate to you, there in the earth plane.

The next principle we think you need to make use of in your lifetime is the assurance that you never enter into any experience without God. Yes, the principle assures you that God is ever present, ever caring. Then why do you live your lives as if you had no one to count on? Why act as though you have nothing to fall back on, that you have no one to help you? The principle IS! The God truth stands! You only have to use the thought process of belief to put it to work in your life.

Those who use this principle every day never find themselves alone or lonely. The God of the Universe brings those people the eternal truth of His Being—total tenderness, energy for working through problems, gentleness that enters any person wanting comfort and caring.

The God of the Universe is too much to express in any book, but the principles will help you to understand that Nature, that Being, that Presence, that wonderful Eternal Truth that enters the world to be used. Therefore, open your mind right now to these principles, and work out ways to make them work in your own life.

These principles are not the same as your own personal truth, understand. The eternal truth, of which the principles are a part, enters the minds of all mankind, whether or not they believe in His presence. But only those who reach out to make use of the principles will find powerful energy that will go to work in their lifetime experiences.

Give yourself time to absorb what we say here. Give yourself time to become the open mind which teams up with these principles that work in your world even now. Those who say they have never heard of such a thing are merely entering into the earth-mind truth. Some say these principles are not principles but the fruits of the godly way of life. Those who preach this unwholesome sermon team up with the erroneous earth-mind which loves to bring God to the level of the worst attributes of earth.

Remember, God does not judge you. The God of the Universe only gives. Therefore, the principle of giving is what you must understand if you are to take advantage of what we present here. Be true to the principle—**God IS the Gift, the Giver, the Absolute Eternal Truth which provides energy to the entire Universal Intelligence of whom you are a part.**

Give yourself time to enter into these thoughts, for they need time, patience, and they need your everlasting willingness to perform "miracles" in your life. When you work slowly, carefully, but steadfastly, these principles will be clear to you. They will be the truth eternal that will hold your own life together.

Now enter into another principle which works in that part of you which houses your spirit. Yes, this principle will help the physical part of you when the spirit part of you turns the principle toward the body. The principle is this: **The world we live in teams up with creative energy that melds itself into total wholeness.** This principle questions each part of the material world, including your body, to give it the new energy of wholeness. This principle will allow no entity to go without healing, and it will help each person to get pure substance (the basic element of all materiality) if needed. This principle insists, in fact, on wholeness everywhere.

Therefore, the principle insists that your own body be whole. Now you wonder at this, we know. You may be wondering if you can team up with more than part of this principle! But if you, the reader, want this principle to work in your life, it will. The thing to do here is NOT to look at others, at other bodies, other worldly creations. The principle is only applicable to the individual who reaches out in mind to make use of it. In this way all principles work.

Healing is part of this principle. Wholeness insists on health. Wholeness insists on purity. Purity insists that earth must undergo its upheaval. The wholeness principle is your eternal truth, your practical way of enjoying the whole body, the whole brain—perfect health.

But not all people want wholeness, you know. Do you? The wholeness principle insists on wholeness in every part of you, remember. If you embrace the principle, you must submit to the total wholeness picture. Give no more excuses because of health. Give no more physical reasons for not doing this thing or not doing that. You will perform perfectly, not imperfectly, and people will come to expect this standard of you. Enter into wholeness, and you forever leave any trifling illnesses or imperfections of your body, and then the greatness of the wholeness principle will team up with you.

Be into our words here, for embracing eternal truth is not a matter of dipping your finger into something good to get a mere taste. It is washing yourself with new open truth and then becoming a new person, indeed. The few will want to be made new; the many will smile and make excuses.

Now then, enter into yet another principle that will be most helpful to you. This principle eternalizes every tender wish that you hold in your heart. "God is love," you say. But we tell you that God is much more than love. **He IS that which rises to your every heartfelt need.** Become one with this understanding: God is Tenderness in Expression. Tenderness is much more than love, reader. Tenderness takes the thought of caring and concern to the ether where everything that bothers your inner being can be healed.

The tenderness principle means that God has presented the totality of His own tenderness to the earth plane. You who think you have no tenderness in your life must reach out to receive this truth. You who think nothing can ever meet your need for affection and love must enter into the truth with energy.

New eternal truth will reveal itself as you meet the challenges in this presentation, but we must rest awhile before we take you further. We think you might not take that last principle into your being with sufficient understanding. Therefore, we rest a moment in order to give you elaboration on this matter.

Tenderness is never understood by mankind, who thinks relationships are all a matter of the give and take of affection. The earth plane reveals no way to make love permanent. Only the principle of tenderness can give that truth to you. Tenderness, as God gives it, enters you from the overflow of His Being. The tender presences, too, team up with you in this spirit of the principle of tenderness. They deal with you out of their tenderness, which again is the overflow of their beings, not the relationship which offers you friendship and takes it away if you disappoint them.

Tenderness, as expressed in the principle, will not need replenishment. It will not need supplementation. It will not require a return! What other truth can hope to satisfy your heartfelt needs any more than this we speak of?

Work awhile with this principle, and before you go on, try your best to give all your resistance (to the tenderness principle) to the winds of the universe which whisk away any negative reaction or thought process in regard to it. Then, when you have summoned this principle into your life to work its good within you, read on.

These principles we have presented here constitute that which we think you need most. We determine this need by the cries we hear from the earth plane, cries that indicate people want what is already theirs—if they only understood how to claim it. Yes, the principles stand firmly in place. Those who understand this truth we present may lay claim to them. The others will wonder what it is all about.

Now we want to team up with you in the truth of the open channel. This truth enters you when you seek the God-mind connection, and it offers you the opportunity of one-on-one counseling, guidance, and one-on-one truth that comes through God-mind just for you.

However, the truth eternal, which pours out for all and is stated here in the principles, teams up with those who understand. The personal truth is one thing; the eternal truth is another. Yet, they are both truth. People who believe in the Universal Presence have no trouble teaming up with eternal truth. Those who have never known of the personal truth, however, will wonder and even doubt the good truth which enters just for them.

To be your full potential, however, to be the one who has power, you must embrace the entire truth—eternal and personal. We name these two kinds of truth in order to help you understand the difference, not to give you hard and fast terms. To understand (the difference) is to hold your mind open to the possibilities, and once you accomplish this insight within yourself, you will then receive full power through the truth which enters you.

We think this chapter opens you to the understanding of the possible truth available to your use. When you master the understanding, when you team up with that which will bring you the teamwork, the open channel and the wisdom, you will be able to survive in whatever condition you find yourself.

"Teteract" Truth—Large Promises, Small Rewards

11

I want to put my God-mind truth into the earth plane as whatever I need. How can I attain this goal?

Unfamiliar words occasionally appear in the material I receive, words that aren't in any English dictionary. One of these words is "teteract," and it is used as an adjective. "Teteract truth never gives satisfaction," the messenger told me. A second word—the antithesis of "teteract"—is "peterstet," also used as an adjective. "Peterstet truth never lets you down," I was told.

The truth we bring through God-mind eternalizes all that is good in the universe. This truth or teamed up good is what people long for and want in their lives. The tenderness with which this truth presents itself is irresistible, and people, therefore, want more and more of it because it perfectly satisfies.

However, the truth which is generally accepted in the earth plane is not what we label **truth.** We call it "teteract truth"—that which teams up with people but never completely satisfies them. This kind of truth puts a thorn in your side because it involves pain and suffering. It promises big rewards, yes, but it never lives up to expectations.

This promise of good misleads many people, for it

opens their hearts but closes their minds. They proceed only with emotion and not reality. The reality we speak of never perishes, for it is made of the stuff of incorruption.

Teamwork with the tender presences will inevitably lead you to worthwhile truth which eternalizes that which is good. But teteract truth will eventually cause you pain. That which wounds is truth that emanates through earth-mind to your mind. It tells you that there is only so much wealth, for example. Then, with your mind fixed on this so-called "fact," you miss the **God principle of truth that says God is not depleted through use; God's wealth increases, not decreases.**

Thorn-in-the-side (teteract) truth seems worthwhile because it teams up with the best in earth thought. Earth-mind truth eternalizes the earth as the producer of wealth, for example, but it pictures man as only a user, not one who replenishes. Therefore, teteract truth is weak, and in the long run, it is unsatisfying.

It provides people with the essence of what begins as truth but ends as the eternalization of negative rewards. Teteract truth pours in and receives power through attention, but it will never bring satisfaction, nor will it bring new and needed God truth into the earth itself. Therefore, it is important to understand that earth truth, which sounds wise and good and pours out from the combined wisdom of mankind, is the thorn-in-the-side or teteract truth.

Be true to your God-mind connection, readers. Team up with those who really know the difference between what is true and what is false, between what is almost truth and what is absolute truth. When you get truth separated in your mind, you will team up with what is eternally powerful and tender beyond belief.

Now we are ready to proceed with the recognition you must develop if you are to thwart that which comes through earth-mind. Team up with this writing and open your mind to our words.

Eternalize what God is. Open your mind still further to enhance your eternalization to one that is open-ended.

This great God concept is the basis of your understanding and will be your touchstone to recognize what is merely earth-mind truth and what is the truth of universal satisfaction.

Once the God of the Universe is opened to your spirit self, you may know the wise, eternal truth that provides you with your every need. But, without this process, you will go on as before, teaming up with earth-mind truth sometimes and other times teaming up with God-mind truth. This dilemma is a powerful obstacle that prevents your growth as an eternalizer who produces God truth in your environment and in your body. It also keeps you from being a teammate who provides truth in expression for everyone.

The New Age requires much more of you than you are now doing. That which has been "good enough" becomes that which will fail in the age to come. That which has met your standards of good for the benefit of mankind will not suffice when the earth turns and trembles. What you will need then is your total God truth that marches to the God-mind drumbeat, that which teams up with substance to become the necessities of life.

Earth-mind truth will never do in the age to be revealed. It will place you in jeopardy physically, and you will not know which way to turn for help. The reason this is true is because the earth will not respond to the old thoughts or the old concepts. The earth will be as a virgin who does not know how to bring forth fruit. You must be the one who plants the seed in this virgin, nourishes it in God truth and then brings it into that which will provide the food supply of the New Age.

The writer thinks there will be seeds in the earth, that all you need do is wait for them to grow! But this will not do at all. The plants of the earth will abound, but where are the ones to provide food? And how do you get a large supply? That is where the understanding of God truth works for you and for many. **Better truth produces better growth**. This principle works now and it will work then.

Though the concept seemed clear enough, I wondered how I

or anyone else could attain the seed to plant. Practical details eluded my understanding, but the messenger from the Brotherhood hastened to explain.

The "practical details" that you mention enter into this truth we talk of. The truth instated within the earth provides the fertile fields. The truth instated within you teams up with what you need, want and desire. The writer still expresses consternation. The way truth works is this—hold out your hand. What seed teams up there? What eternal truth puts the seed in your hand? Why, God truth puts it there.

I asked, "Am I supposed to be holding a seed in my hand?"

There is no particular need at this moment, is there? Then why be amazed that you hold no seed?

True, I needed no seed at the moment I was writing. But shouldn't I practice? I waited for illumination.

Truth must be used, Truth-giver, not played with. That which you now do is playful, not given to serious work. What do you see as need? What do you want the truth to do in your world, in you? To manifest truth, eternalize the whole God concept, not just part of it. Team up with your tender presences, and hold out the truth you need at the present moment.

I sat quite still in front of the word processor screen. If I or the readers are to manifest truth, why can't we practice? The patient communicator explained.

There is practice and there is need. To practice is to seek things because you want to stand before others as successful, not because you want to meet needs. Where is the generous God thought? Where is the perfect eternalization that will help others? A seed of corn in your hand is worth nothing! The thought process that works to bring you or anyone else into the perfect manifestation of truth is what is important. Therefore, we say to you and to others that you must use truth NOW, but use it according to the needs you perceive. The writer has no real need for seed, no greatness to manifest. She has no garden plot, no field to till, no multitude to feed.

Team up, for now, with the process. Then we will lead

you further in the process until you do manifest whatever it is that you need to call forth to the betterment of the earth and to the enhancement of mankind.

The New Testament tells the story of the first "miracle" that Jesus is supposed to have performed—the transforming of water into wine. I asked if the same principle of God truth applies to the wine as would apply to the seed or any other practical need.

The truth applied to the transforming of water to wine was the one Jesus used to put God truth into motion. First, he held the thought that God is too great to be encompassed in one mind. Second, Jesus entered the eternalization of wine in the jars. He teamed up with the idea of good wine because God is only capable of putting good into motion. Finally, Jesus gave his truth to others who opened their minds to his eternalization.

The seed you would need to plant in the field will come forth as the wine came forth because the God truth is the God truth each and every time, not just sometimes if and whenever He decides to act. Therefore, count on the seed.

Quite unnecessarily, I'm sure, I reminded the advanced spirit who writes through me that Jesus' followers then and now said he performed miracles so that people would believe in him as the Christ.

It is true that people turn the idea of what Jesus did to their point of view. But they question the very nature of God when they do this. **Jesus came to show people how to make use of the Father God in their daily lives**, but most did not understand. They turned away from the concept Jesus taught and made Jesus God Himself.

The way to perform the same "miracles" that Jesus performed is to apply the same principles! We say this to you over and over. God truth is not hidden; it is not secreted in the rocks; it is not illuminated by a very few self-proclaimed teachers who go about telling others what and who Jesus really is.

The truth of earth-mind proclaims itself as God; here is the travesty! Here is the eternal wretchedness that leads people astray! The truth that is eternal is that which pours forth only to those who turn their ears to hear. The **peterstet** truth is that which satisfies. The **teteract** truth only puts a thorn in your side.

Now then—right the wrong of earth truth by teaming up with the principle we teach here, **the principle of God, your partner, who works through you to give you all good gifts**. When you put this principle into your eternal being, you will then right the wrong of earth truth.

Believe in the works of Jesus, those of you who reach out in the perspective of his followers. Reach not only into the works of Jesus, but reach also into the works of others who turned to God-mind for their wisdom. The entities who voice their loyalty to the Christian ethic open their minds only to the ethic, not to the God Who eternalized the good that Jesus performed before those who knew him in the earth plane.

Those who led their people as Jesus led people—by example and by the wisdom of God expressed in his lifetime experience—teamed up with God, not with man. Their legacies enter the truth into the earth, but their followers tend to dissipate that truth by corrupting acts and eventual disregard of what the person originally told them all through the lifetime experience.

No truth enters when you turn only to those entities who empty their words upon you to persuade you of their interpretations of what God IS, what God wants, what God is eternalizing. They enter to harangue and to bring their own viewpoints to those who give them heed. The result, for those who give their minds over to such opinions, is that the great individual potential is reduced to commonplace acts which hold no true wisdom.

You and you only must be the center of power when you open your mind to God and allow His gifts to pour through you to enter into your life experience. These words we give you open to your mind and give you new awareness. Team up with them.

The touchstone is God Himself, remember. The way you prove either teteract truth or peterstet truth is to use your God concept to end the wondering. God will team up only with **His** truth, remember. That which is earth-mind empties itself on you and is persuasive because so many give it temporary power. Therefore, wrest the truth of God to your being and leave no room for inferior teteract truth.

To put this subject into terms that you and I can manage a day at a time, I asked the spirit entity from the Brotherhood of God to show us how to make use of God truth right now. I sensed a shaking of heads as the answer came.

This writer has asked this question many, many times. Yet, she wonders how to use it day by day! We explain; she writes it down; yet, she still wonders! However, we will team up with her again to write it down, to try to explain what is apparently not easy for some to accept.

God truth is that which is the ultimate in truth. Though there are other truths around, none of them will sustain you forever. These other truths will eventually let you down and leave you despondent, ill or disappointed in life. Therefore, the reason God truth gives you perfect teamwork is that it is the truth of wisdom, the truth of the Teammate, God. No better way of explaining its value is possible!

Now—hold your mind on this Partner, the God of the Universe. Get the picture, the picture of the open-ended God. Feed your soul this picture until your soul, your spirit self, cannot think of anything except God. Be into the understanding that you and God are One, not two. Never hold out the probability that it is you who generates the power. God generates; you only open the way to let Him prove His Being in your life. Fix your mind upon this Giver of Gifts, this Gift in and of Himself, this Perfection, this Wholeness, this Eternalization of Tenderness.

The way is paved; the path is clear. The river holds no rocks to snag your boat. Why wait? The day is not yet over, reader. The day holds the possible teamwork of you, God and this Brotherhood in its potential. Use the Gift; team up with us; hold the clear God truth in your being. What is the need? What is the truth you want to manifest? Enter into this work now, not later. Put the truth to work in your world now.

The truth that holds no wavering teamwork, the truth that knows no wrong, the truth that puts forth what it promises is that which you want in your life—none other. Here lies the thrust of our message. Here lies the purpose for which we speak to you of teteract truth or thorn-in-the-side truth. You must know which truth to enter into; you must understand the worth of each; you must know how to work day by day to provide your being with what it needs and wants to become its potential in this lifetime.

New Age Teamwork

12

How can I survive and enjoy the New Age without the necessities of life?

Those who will work to help reduce pain and suffering in the New Age are now being teamed up with new ways of overcoming problems. Those who reduce pain will become one with the Pure Truth that allows them to lead others to eventual good. The reader of this book may well be one of these who will help others to survive and prosper.

The New Age has many requirements that mankind does not dream of now. Those who want to survive into this Age must know how to present the truth within them to the substance which will convert into material solutions. Those who put this Pure Truth first in their lives will not want for any of the necessities of life. They will enter into the teamwork of the Tender Teammate Who is God, Who is that Presence universal, that Truth eternal, that Good eternal.

Now, direct your thoughts to this chapter only if you feel ready to embark on the adventure called "The New Age Teamwork." You who have indicated your willingness to become God's teammates are now ready to open your minds to the Pure Truth needed to survive and to enjoy the New Age. Therefore, read this chapter with the pleasure of one who is about to embark on a glorious voyage to places unknown and unseen.

Perfect eternalizations must be forthcoming if you will put your Pure Truth into operation to become the material worth. That which opens itself to your need will do so only if the perfect truth enters the substance which then opens itself to the material. The teamwork needed to make this come about can be used by those who want and need certain things.

Manifesting truth into material form is not the miraculous thing many people think it is. The way to accomplish this process is to empty yourself of previous thoughts as to how things may be put on earth. If you persist in believing that earth produces that which has value, then you will not make use of the process we now explain. The way, then, to put yourself beyond the thrust of earth truth is to get rid of the old thoughts.

What do you think of when you need to eat? The refrigerator, perhaps? The grocery store? The garden already planted and now in harvest? These are the usual thoughts, are they not? But we say to you, to prepare yourself for the New Age, you must put other sources into your picture of how you may meet your needs.

That which belongs to you is yours. This truth is one that you need to examine with infinite concern. The eternalization of what is actually yours is needed if you are to claim what is yours. If you cannot cement the eternalization clearly within your mind, then you cannot make the claim. Become clear in your mind that what we tell you here is absolutely true. No eternalization can be vague, uncertain or of no consequence. That which you claim for your own will come to you if the eternalization is clear.

Team up now to review what we have already told you about the process to claim your own, whatever "your own" might be. First, team up with those in this plane, your tender presences, who can help you. Second, present your very open mind that has no preconceived ideas of how this process will work. Hold only the thought that the statement of truth is absolutely correct—**that which belongs to you is yours.**

Third, turn to the place where you team up with the One who is open to your every thought, your every need, your every truth. This One we call God. The God you know must be entirely open ended, as we have told you before. Then the teamwork will prosper.

The tender presences will be there to help you step by step with the process which will very soon become almost instantaneous with you. They will lead you, steady your vision, keep you into the truth needed to accomplish the process.

It may seem easy for you to hold the clear eternalization in your mind. The fact is, it is easier for some than it is for others. There are many reasons why this is so, but we won't go into them right now. Suffice it to say that the eternalization of the need must be very, very clear.

The writer wants us to give some example here. So that you may be entirely clear in this matter, we will open the process to you through the story of one who has made use of it in his earth life.

Team up with eternal truth in the matter of the entity who entered earth life to become an eternalizer of good. This individual gave his truth to all, to people with great need, to the earth which had lost its teamwork with good, to the forward growth of his own spirit self and the spirit selves of others, too.

This entity entered the earth in a place where a food supply was scarce, where people had very little in the way of possessions to prosper their lives. He, however, teamed up with the One he perceived was the Power Center of the Universe. He saw no good to speak of in the place where he lived, but very early in life he turned to this Power Center of the Universe with full expectation of the material things that he needed and wanted, and he gave these things his attention.

No one around him thought him to be very sane, of course. What person goes forth in the morning to produce his needs and wears no look of pain and suffering?

Who goes forth to open the door to riches and does not expect to wrestle the powerful beings in earth? Who opens his door to give what he has freely and without reservation, not even expecting the receivers to pay him in some way or to become his debtors? No one understood this person because people rooted themselves in the expectations of earth truth. This individual, however, heard the true drum beat, the true marching song, and he went out early in the morning to claim what was his.

You can be like this person. The time approaches when you must team up with this process if you are to enter the New Age with confidence. That which is yours is to be claimed, not pushed aside. That which belongs to you is yours to claim because none other can claim it for you. Think on this matter with true intent, with great energy and with even greater expectation.

The way to claim your riches is **not** to enter into the idea of nothingness. The writer seeks to answer the question of what to do with your mind when you claim what is yours in the universal substance. Your mind must be held to its purpose, for it is your key, your means to the accomplishment of good. But even this understanding is not enough to bring the process to its conclusion.

To enter into the process, do what we say, not what you might like to think we say. There is a difference. We say what we mean, but your thoughts center on what you **think** we mean here. We do not mean that you must become the holy of holies in the eyes of mankind. How foolish is such a thought. God IS. God does not survey you to see if you are deserving.

Be! Be! Do you understand what we mean? No? Well, "Be" means that you simply must be whatever it is you are without posturing in any way. There is no need for groveling, no need of teaming up with a public demonstration of your piety. Be! God meets you where you are—not in some far place where you think you ought to be. God Is what He Is! You must be whatever you are.

"Be" means that your being is whatever it is because of the many lifetimes you have lived. Therefore, rest in that thought. The person who you are in this lifetime is only one such expression of your being, not the total expression. Therefore, you do not even know your real self in your conscious thought. You see, touch and experience life in one body at a time, and therefore, you know not what you truly are, right?

Being the person you are takes some thought on your part, but you must spend this time if you are to be one who uses Pure Truth in the way we have described in this chapter. Therefore, think on the matter. Accept yourself as having lived many lifetimes trying to become one with God. Yes, that is the purpose of these lifetimes. When you become one with God, you enter into the perfect freedom of expression that allows no restriction upon you.

Give yourself these thoughts as you study the matter of who you are. When you can accept yourself in this way, **Be!** Team up with this entity, you, and then proceed to get the rest of your house in order.

The writer expresses a question about how a human being can divorce himself or herself from the idea that the earth produces our food, for example. This entity is hard into the idea that all material comes through the material itself. The trees provide paper. The fields produce harvest. But yet what has produced the trees? What has produced the fields, the seeds to plant therein? In this way think it through. There must be a center or nucleus that produces whatever is. What is that center, that nucleus?

You might say piously and without understanding, "Why, God makes it all."

Then, you may expect powerful energy to act on your behalf because you gave the right answer! That will not happen, reader. That will not happen, writer of this book. You are far afield when you think in this manner. The way to team up with the process is to go step by step, and if that does not work, divide the steps into steps. Understand? That process of understanding is not easy to accomplish, not easy to become one with. Be into our explanation.

Team up now with this idea of creating the right process within you so that you may use it at will in the physical world. To begin, give no concerned thought to the world you live in. Think of yourself in space, floating. The world is far away and you view it without any particular emotion. What it is, where it is, how it exists is no concern to you. The Teammate we have told you of, the great God of the Universe or Intelligence or Mind—whatever you wish to call that which is the power behind existence—is there in space for you. Put your ear to the heartbeat. Put your eye to the gentle loveliness. Then open your being like a rose unfolding to this Greatness. Gentle warmth pervades you. The gentle Teammate holds you to His Being. The Pure Truth pours through you.

You now look out at planet earth, blue and white, seemingly floating without plan. You observe it for awhile. Then you know without words or articulated thought that the earth out there is in the operation of Higher Intelligence, in the powerful understanding of the God of the Universe. Therefore, the planet takes on more interest to you, for you, too, are in the operative control of this same Greatness. The two of you—entity and planet—give yourselves over to whatever you name the Divine Presence.

Now—ready? The planet earth receives its power and sustenance from the same source your being receives its power and sustenance. The Truth Eternal is yours now. God—Divine Intelligence, the Truth in Expression, the God whom you name in whatever way or whatever form—is part of the powerful Center that produces whatever is upon the planet and whatever is within you. That Power Center is what you focus on until you hold this truth within you forever.

The writer is seeking her own answers. Her questions enter those tender presences who want to help her and you to understand. She wants to know if God Is regardless of whether she acknowledges this fact or not. "Will

God," she wants to know, "team up with me and the earth even if there is no acknowledgment of Him?" Is the sun still the sun even though the earth turns? Eternal truth is eternal truth no matter if people or planet recognize it. Therefore, you may wonder, why bother to understand that God is God?

The answer is that if you are to make use of this divine Teammate to produce the truth in material form, you must understand that God—Divine Presence, Intelligence, Universal Truth—is the power you may use to produce good. There are many analogies, of course. The Father God is one analogy that presents a God who protects, cares about and provides for you. The only problem with this concept is that people tend to use it in superficial ways and create a God patterned after earthly fathers. And this picture will not do at all!

Therefore, we prefer the approach we gave you before—the thought of you and the earth in space with the understanding penetrating you that your being and the earth itself is prospered by the Great Force or Power Center of the Universe that we call God or some other equally giant expression of universality.

The process seems difficult, you think? New ways of thinking always require a great wrenching inside the entity making the change. Therefore, persevere. In a short time you will have the understanding required, and you will marvel, as we do, that it ever seemed hard. You will want to explain it to others, but they may turn deaf ears or give you wary looks. "But," you say to them, "this way of thinking will enable you to send your thoughts right into substance!" They will smile and perhaps say it seems wonderful, but they will still turn away.

The operative requirement for this teamwork that will make you the controller of your world and your being, is that you open your mind to this process. Before you team up with it, think carefully step by step until your mind revels in the process. Then you will know you are ready to perform.

We do not mean "perform" in the sense of a stage performance, of course. We recommend that you team up with the tender presences to let them help you along, and then perform whatever it is that you need without an audience. Those involved will wonder how such a thing came about, but you, if you will resist self-glorification, will shake your head. Then, when the process is easy to comprehend and to use, you will tell others of it as you go along, hoping to help them do likewise. The more people who can use the process, the better will be the New Age! That makes sense, doesn't it?

The writer wonders, however momentarily, if the process could be used to control others. Remember what we have told you earlier? The God concept is totally good, totally generous. That open-ended concept of God will allow no selfish use of the process, for you team up with good in order to work it through.

The writer asks if the work ethic taught on earth is in conflict with what we give you here in the way of producing your thoughts into substance. The work ethic implied in our process is that of adherence to the principle of truth, not the earth truth that promises what it cannot deliver. The earth-mind tells you that if you work hard and steadily that you will succeed in prosperity. But many work hard and find that the ethic does not work for them. It does not mean that the earth truth of working hard is wrong; it merely means that it does not go far enough. Such is the way of all earth truth; it does not go the distance required.

Now we leave you with much to think about, much to work through to understand. In the next chapter we will tell you how to use this process right now and how to work with the Teammate to put good truth into the earth.

The Case
For Non-Judgment
13

Why isn't my judgment of truth and of God helpful to my spiritual growth and to my role as a teammate?

That which is true, that which is open to God-mind, that which pours out to you through the open channel will make your life wonderful indeed. The best way to appreciate these words is to rest in the thought that God gives you what is His to give not because you are perfect or even near perfect, but He gives what is His to give **because His nature is to give**.

Because God is a Giver of good gifts, you enter into teamwork with Him to receive all that your mind can open to. Though it seems simple, perhaps, to think of God as a Giver, apparently many people enter into a different kind of thinking altogether. They think of God as they think of people, and they enter into wrong thoughts which hold back their progress. Because they know people who are vindictive, people who sow seeds of distrust or hate, they believe the God Giver must be like them! Oh, they would say differently, of course. But in their hearts they think God is only what they see people being.

What short-sighted, discouraging and destructive thoughts these are! To make use of the God of the Universe, the Giver of good gifts, the Teammate Who enters to help you become your potential, you must open your spirit self to the God truth which will reorganize your life into the open-ended potential that will lead you to greatness in this lifetime.

Now eternalize with this writer what it is you want to bring into your life. This eternalization is received within your inner temple where it rests in the pure light of God. By putting what you desire within this temple, you awaken it to what it is in reality and what it can be potentially. The entity that you are, therefore, can become one with the perfect outpicturing of that stated desire. To produce this picture into the materiality of earth, you must enter into the eternal truth that God provides for everyone.

The truth pours in and tells you that nothing is impossible, nothing is too great to achieve, that what you want to occur in your life is for the greater good, not only for you but for all. This is the way it works, the entering truth that helps your desire become an earth reality.

Gentle presences, advanced spirits from the Brotherhood of God, team up with you and give you counsel on how to produce whatever it is that is now pictured within you. They send their powerful thoughts to you, and you who have now become proficient in communication, open your mind to them. They enter and the work begins.

The tender presences may speak to you about the Pure Truth, that which is yours and yours alone and is that which you must heed. You, if open and receptive, will understand that this Pure Truth is not brought to you because it is beautiful or good. No! It is brought to you because it is the truth you need to work with. Your open mind will then begin to work with it.

The positive thrust of God puts this Pure Truth into your being where you must work with it to perform it in your life. Then that Pure Truth belongs to you and becomes part of the reality of you. The writer wants us to give an example.

The person who knows that he wants God to help him

produce the best thought that he has teams up with the open channel. He says, "The thought form that I want to see projected into my life is one of great prosperity. The way I see it, tender presences, is that if I had plenty of money, I would be free to give my time to doing good."

"No!" comes the reply. "You are teamed up with erroneous thinking here. What teams up with you is not the picture of prosperity, but the thought of becoming the omnipotent one who can be seen by men in his do-gooding!"

The individual then protests and states that he only wants to help others, that he sees the needs, but he hasn't the time or the money to help all those needs he perceives in his world. Therefore, if his personal problem is solved, he can devote himself to the good works that he most fervently wants to do.

"Be gone," we say to one who enters with selfish wants! "Be gone," we say to the one who has no real understanding of generosity or of tenderness within him! This entity has lost the God concept, you see, the God concept that perceives that **God Is**, not **God might be persuaded.** The God this one sends his thoughts to is a copy of people he knows, perhaps a copy of his father or mother on earth.

The way to demonstrate is not to put God in that temporary box you brought along for that purpose, but to put God where He Is—in the truth that pervades the universe and which holds the planets in their orbits. Who could expect to bargain with such a concept of God?

Team up today with the understanding that what we bring you through God-mind is that God is not that which your own thought waves produce. God Is the all in all, the best and the greatest, the most and the potential, the entire Whatever Is that you can only partially perceive. This concept, then, is open ended enough to enter into your thinking mind.

To even entertain the idea of being the teammate who eternalizes thoughts which get the cooperation of God, you must be open enough **not to formulate ideas** but **to**

receive them through the open channel which opens to you. When you formulate ideas of your own about what God Is or Is Not, you are becoming the judge. This position will limit your performance as demonstrator and will put you with those who open themselves to the least when they might have the best.

Become those who offer no judgment of what God Is. That kind of judgment offers nothing of value to you in the living of your life. That kind of judgment prohibits the power of the great Teammate from operating in your life. When you limit God, you limit what He can do through you. The analogy to this is the valve that you may open or shut down depending on what kind of flow you want. To get the maximum flow, you open it fully.

Here, then, is the way to promote God truth in your life. Team up with the tender presences who stand at the ready. Then speak to them of your life, whatever seems to be troubling you, whatever seems to be holding you back. Team up with them in this way without making demands or without having expectations. The demands and the expectations only close the valve, because they once again judge what the response will be.

Never put your judgment upon the response from either the tender presences or from God. Open the valve without fear of the flow diminishing. Remember—whatever is of God only increases with use, not diminishes. Be teamed up now with what we say. Review, if you need to. Tender presences stand by to help you put this together.

Your personal truth is given you because you open yourself to the eternalization of its worth. Therefore, we urge you to be open, not judgmental, in your approach to the truth that pours through to you. When you put yourself in the position of being the judge of whether it is worthwhile or not, you proclaim yourself as the invincible truth, not God-mind. Then you will diminish the worth of both eternal and personal truth to the point that you receive very little of value.

People enter into truth, but they often eternalize such

narrow valve openings that only the tiniest amount seeps through to them. They have the idea that when God speaks, that truth must be handled like poison that is dangerous! Why shut down the flow? Why? Because the entire open flow of truth must be dangerous! That is the way the eternalization seems to be performed by too many in the earth plane.

Those who empty themselves of judgment enter into the teamed up truth freely, quickly and without anguish. They enter their open minds into this tremendous and powerful flow and become the ones to benefit quickly. They enter into perfect truth, perfect for them. That is the way it must be if you, who are different from your neighbor, are to prosper and proclaim the potential that is yours for the seeking.

Become one who sends the beggar truth of earth into nothingness, for the truth of earth has neither lasting value nor even temporary worth. Hold the eternalization of openness upon your mind, hold it there, and then claim what is certainly yours. Given these facts, why would you hesitate?

Because this writer thinks we need to be very precise, we will now attempt to test this truth we bring. Those of you who feel ready to test your potential growth may team up with us to enter into this better way of becoming the teammates of God.

The open channel provides you with the means of communication. Team up with this channel. Then send your thoughts to the tender presences that you want to learn how to demonstrate what is good, what is desirable and whatever the world needs. These who ready themselves to help will begin the teaching.

New thoughts, new truth will pour through the open channel until you thrust it away from you because your mind has too much to hold in one setting. Then retire from the channel. Take notes either at this point or while the inpouring truth comes to you. Review your notes. Think on their meaning and grasp what you can. That which you still question hold up again to the tender presences that they may illuminate you. Enter into this process again and again, as much as you desire, until you prepare yourself for the truth that will become material.

Teaming up with those tender presences will be the way to enter into effective communication, at least in the beginning. The open channel is not closed to you—ever! Those who stand by to help you will be there for you night and day because they want to help you always. Therefore, never hesitate because of the hour. There is no night in the next plane of life. The point is—when you open your mind to those who assist you, they will open to you with good thoughts concerning your request.

Being the ones who enter with the good truth, they will never be opinionated or judgmental. They understand how judgment fixes the thought process in cement and hurts open channel communication. These advanced spirits only offer help to you who want help. They want what you want—oneness with the God of the Universe.

Gentle thoughts will persist as you open your mind. These thoughts will help you to work through the problems in your life, whatever they are. There is no problem that cannot be tackled in the light of God-mind. These entering spirits will eternalize your good within them and help you to understand the entering truth.

Now—go with those presences who enter to help you. Team up with them that they may be your friends who want your life to reach its potential good. What more can you want? This is the time, reader, when you become the entity who enters into the personal truth that will set you free of all the problems you now believe you have. Team up. Team up.

Prosperity
Through God-Mind

14

How will I get food, shelter and clothing when the earth begins to shift on its axis?

Prosperity consists of having what is needed, what is wanted, what is desired. That you may truly be prosperous, we will now present this chapter in two parts. The first part brings to your understanding the God Who is wealth, the God Who brings His good gifts to you and says to you, "Take." The second part brings you the needed principles by which you can understand true prosperity, by which you can understand why God IS the Perfect Giver.

No doubt most of you call prosperity money. However, those of you who have read other material about the true nature of prosperity have widened your understanding of prosperity to anything that acts to prosper your life. You understand how you are prospered with the great truth of the open channel, and you know this truth prospers your soul growth. You also understand that your friendships, which give you deep tenderness, also prosper you. To find great friendships, hold to God truth, hold to the teamwork which will help you to bring into your life whatever is needed. Physical needs must also be expressed if you are truly prosperous. Put the thought that says, "Physical things are not godly," out the window of your inner temple. That you who express in physical form could be prosperous without manifesting what is physical is truly unthinkable. You want things because you, too, are material and because you have basic needs.

Basic needs are not always those needs that arise out of desperation. They are also those things that would make life easier and brighter. These have their place alongside food, shelter and clothing. That which opens you to much teamwork with God will prosper you beyond your greatest hopes. Your best thoughts or eternalizations will produce whatever you deem wanting in your life, not just those things that are "basic necessities."

Bring new thought into play here. The "how" of demonstration has been discussed elsewhere; therefore, now we will discuss making your selection of what to bring into the material world. This discussion may seem unnecessary to some of you. Why, after all, discuss what to make visible? Why not manifest everything you think of —every thought of need and desire?

A selection process is necessary because if you try to bring it all into the worldly framework, you will lose the power of producing thought into things. The key word here is **discrimination**. The selection process is only the eternal truth understood and put into play. That which is of God, the Teammate, is what you truly want to bring into the visible. **The Teammate enters into the process because He is the Power that turns the thought into materiality.** This eternal truth is real, practical, and it is the hope for your demonstrations. It operates, as all eternal truth operates, by principle. (See Chapter 12.)

Never put into operation the idea that you, on your own, can put thought into the visible material world. The Teammate is needed. Therefore, because He is needed, He must be part of the selection process. That is the way the principle works. Those of you who now back off because this seems too complicated, must review what the

114

"God Eternal" means.*

Thought performed in the marketplace is God's teamwork made visible. That which you bring about with your own power is accomplished because of your work, your striving. That part you understand easily. The difficulty, of course, is understanding that there is this wonderful way of producing your thought into things by teaming up with God. Because this understanding seems new, many lose their way here. But if you stay with us, enter into the work we want entered, you will be the open mind that makes thoughts into things with ease.

We want to teach you what is worthwhile. We want to explain how thought turns itself into a good expression of prosperity. You want to be teamed up with plenty of good gifts, no doubt. What do you have in mind? You may play with first one idea and then another, but the one idea that will work because it must is the one that reflects the biggest concept of the God of the Universe that you can accept. The only way to bring an eternalization into full demonstration is to rework the idea through the Mind of God.

Turn to God-mind through the open channel. Team up with the one who reaches out to you with the nature of Goodness, Perfection, Tenderness, of Teamwork. This Greatness will work with you when you rest the thought to be projected in the truth that now opens to you. That which honors God rests easily with the inner self, and it has no doubting thoughts. That which rests easily and steadily within you must be that which God knows is right and good. It is true—the goodness and the right-

---

* The term "God eternal" is explained by the Brotherhood. The "God Eternal" opens to the reader's mind as he or she reaches out to encompass the larger concept of God. Those who open to a larger God concept will have no trouble with this term, but others may need to review it with those presences who stand ready to teach you whatever you need to know to bring greater understanding into your mind.

eousness of God must go into the expression of yourthought form. A thought which might hurt someone else or which might cause spiritual uneasiness will not produce.

That which teams up with the God concept, that which opens itself as the Pure Truth will undoubtedly team up with the Power of the Universe. That is what we mean when we say that first, you must let the request undergo the test of God, the Teammate, before you can actually use God power to wrest the thought from the ether and out into the material. The way to use the power that is free to you is to practice discrimination.

The writer wants us to mention that when you leave the earth plane and come to this plane you need to gain control of your thoughts or you will produce such a variety of things around you that you will be frightened. The mind must be disciplined, organized, and above all it must learn to practice God-discrimination.

The next part of the chapter is devoted to enlisting your mind/spirit in the work of turning the God thought that now exists within your mind into the material world. Team up!

The way to put these true thoughts into the material world is to make certain you team up with the One Who eternalizes the All Good principle. "What does this mean?" you may ask. **The God of the Universe, as we have said over and over, is only capable of producing good.** Therefore, that understanding eternalizes the God thought that is worthy of this principle. The way to produce what is purely of God—the perfect thought for the time and the place—is to rest in the principle we have stated.

Think on this principle. Hold it up for examination. Team up with it wholly. Then, and then only, will you be ready to produce! Tenderness surrounds you because the God of the Universe produces what is good in the material form that you hold in your mind. The ether teams up with the substance that produces all that is. There it is! It stands forth in its actuality, its practicality, its full beauty, depending on what it is that you have sent forth to be accomplished.

The perfection of this process is painstaking until you work with it, but when you accomplish it several times, you will team up with whatever is needed or desired as fast as the speed of thought.

Now, we understand that many of you smile here and wonder if what we say is only for those who are susceptible but not too bright! The reason you wonder thusly is that you have submerged your thought process in the earthly reasoning which proclaims that the Pure Truth is proved only by scientific processes. That which eventually becomes material began as material—isn't that the way your thought goes? That which produces thought is different from that which produces the materiality—isn't that what you are thinking?

When you hold these thoughts of science—that study that is only imperfect at best—as the only study with the facts about the world, you limit what is brought to you in this book as beyond the point of scientific knowledge. Why hold yourself back? Why wait for all that we say to be proved? Why think that we must prove to you that what we say is possible?

Those who wait for proof will drag into the New Age with nothing of value to help you or others! You will only have at your command those thoughts of earth truth that will not produce anything except by the hard way—time and hard work! Why wait? Why wait to see others do what we say? Do these seeming miracles on your own.

Because each reader is unique, we can only address you in the general, not the specific. That you may receive individual instruction you must go to the tender presences who will help you to understand. They who know your spirit self will help you to address your doubts, to address your strengths, to make the demonstrations that you must make if you will have the prosperity you desire both now and in the New Age to come.

General help will take you to the point where you must take a leap of teamwork into the eternal truth whether or not you understand it perfectly. The tender presences, however, will bridge that leap. They will help you to cross the gap between doubt and belief without fear. Those who help you never thrust themselves upon you, remember. They stand at the ready; they hold themselves in alertness; they hover here in this plane of life waiting to be called to your plane. Therefore, speak the word. Tell them you are ready to be helped. They enter with wings of truth, with positive teamwork, with every good word that will speak to your unique reality.

Nothing that enters to help will do otherwise. There are many who have fearful beliefs about the spirits of those in this plane. No entity here can hurt you even if one wished to hurt you. The only way to turn your inadequate truth into eternal truth is to open yourself fully to God-mind and let the tender presences help you.

In the New Age there will be many needs to express into satisfying materiality. Basic necessities such as water, food, shelter and even clothing must be brought into the material earth plane, and these needs can be met in the way we have already described. After basic needs are met, there will be other needs such as gaining perfection in both body and in mind. There will be a need for leadership, for bringing positive understanding into the ongoing life, into organization and how to bring what is good into life, the good that makes life worthwhile and happy. All this will be possible if you learn and use the method we give you in this book. The New Age is not to be feared in any way if you understand the prospering ways of putting truth to work in your world.

I asked my correspondent if this earth has ever met any situation similar to the earth's shift upon its axis, and if so, how did people handle it?

The earth has never known complete renewal as it will this time. There have been on-going renewals. There have been many times when the earth acted to become more pure, more given over to its truth, but never has there been a total global upheaval. The change of poles is the question, perhaps. There was a change of poles another time, but it came before there were people to enter into the events.

I tried to picture earth in its new condition, and I could not. I asked for more facts.

Facts, as you call them, are not what you want. The facts will be depressing to the human condition because the earth will undergo a total change in becoming new. Nothing that now stands will stand then. The earth will be teamed up with total renewal. The way people will survive at all is to know where they may go to ride out the storm so to speak. They will take what they can on their backs, they will hold their truth like a lamp, and they will team up with their tender presences who will watch over them while they sleep and advise them when they awake. That is how people will survive.

Those who ride out the storm will then use their truth to manifest those basic needs that stand out in the minds of all who live in the human body. They will turn to the practical use of truth and hold out their best eternalizations of housing, food, the very clothes they wear. Then they will be able to think clearly about how to organize themselves to work with the earth which will now produce good growth once again.

Teamwork will bring people through—teamwork with the generous eternal truth that opens them to the total God concept, open-ended and true to What Is. Therefore, we bring these truth books to you that you may prepare yourself for the time which will come before long. No, the date is not in our knowledge, but the great heaving breaths of the earth tell us that the entire plan of renewal will take place before much longer. Therefore, prepare yourself, reader, and know that God is Truth Personified, Truth which is the Perfection, the Entity Who teams up with you to bring you prosperity that you want in your life now and in the New Age.

Be among those who heed this message, not those who merrily go their ways unheeding and uncertain. None will be brought to destruction who want to survive. None will enter into suffering who want to have good thoughts manifested in their lives. No one, reader, not you or those you love, will be cast out if you will learn the truth about how to put your prosperous thoughts into the earth materiality.

Gentle thoughts now go to you, especially you who persist in thinking fearful thoughts. Remember, there is no death, no destruction of what is your reality. Nothing changes that truth. That which is of God—and you are entirely produced from God thought—will remain the tenderness expressed as you. Not even the renewal of the earth changes the truth of your reality. Therefore, thoughts of your death are erroneous. Eternalize as one who lives throughout the ages.

Be assured, dear reader, that we who give this message will work with you who want to produce whatever is needed for good living, both in the now and in the New Age. Team up with us. Enter into this plan that we present that you may know the total eternalization of how to work with God truth to produce matter.

Within the Circle
of Total Good

15

*How can I be sure to manifest only those things and those
conditions which are for the good of all?*

---

*In the previous chapter the messenger from the Brotherhood
spoke of the "all-good principle" and how we may apply it to
gain prosperity now and in the New Age. This chapter
reemphasizes this principle and takes the reader a step further
into the understanding of Who and What God Is. Yet, though
much is said about God, there is no attempt to define or con-
struct a concept that we can memorize and use.*

*We receive, in this chapter, the essence of what God Is
coupled with an understanding of our relationship with
whatever we call the Highest and the Best in the Universe.
The practical point of this discussion is to help us to learn how
to demonstrate those things in life that are completely good—
and completely of God.*

Again, from the Brotherhood:

Nothing that exists in your mind is open to
judgment—yours, ours or God's. Your mind contains
whatever teams up with whatever you perceive as truth.
Therefore, the thrust of this message is this—to produce
what is good is to align yourself with that Good, that Perfection, that eternalization of Pure Truth that must enter
through God-mind.

To transform a good thought into an actual object that you hold or otherwise manifest, you must turn yourself absolutely toward the Good that exists in this entire universe and beyond. There is, at the basis of the creation you are witness to, the Basic Good which promotes every good, creative idea into the substance of materiality. The science behind this idea is that the beginning point of every created thing, be it mineral, vegetable or animal, eternalizes itself into the ether that operates in the creative process.

Therefore, if you, with your open mind and your God-mind truth instated within you, can team up with this understanding, you know that whatever triggers the thought, that whatever teams up with that Basic Element, will inevitably be produced into the world where you live.

This explanation is not easy, perhaps, to take into your understanding. This is our best truth, however, that will bring the Good into manifestation.

Teaming up with the Basic Element is not to be your concern, however. We tell you of the principle to remind you that God is the Order of the Universe. That which brings all that is into order is that which we now refer to as God, as the Power That Eternalizes, as That Which Produces Whatever Is. The eternalization that is yours to produce is what you must be concerned with.

The Basic Element is of God—of Good, of Perfection. The persuasive power that transforms it into tangible earth substance is the Teammate, the God of the Universe. The One Who Is eternalizes whatever is good, whatever is perfect. Therefore, when you put this One, this Greatness, in the seat of power, you produce whatever it is that you want to produce. This is the way we must explain the teamwork of the entering Pure Truth that is God, the Teammate.

There are those who read this book and wonder at what we say. They have been taught this or that religious belief that teaches them one way and one way only. To be true to your own truth, however, is to turn away from those who teach you this or that religious persuasion. Team up with God-mind and receive your own perfect truth.

By receiving your own truth, you will open to that which enters directly for you, and you will find it irresistible. That which is of God, that which is opening to your own spirit, will allow you to understand our explanations of how to be aligned with the Good (Pure Truth) that prepares you to make perfect demonstrations.

Now to the situation at hand—the New Age which will need your many exhibitions of eternal truth put to practical use. To become ready to attend to your needs and the needs of others, take time now to put this entire concept into interaction with your present life. Yes, we want you to begin now. There is no limit on the number of times you can demonstrate truth! Remember, that to partake of God's gifts is to renew the Source, not to deplete it.

The writer has a hard time with demonstration although she has made demonstrations. The demonstration of the books now in print is the certainty of what we tell you. This writer sends her thoughts toward us to remind us that she wants to demonstrate, but she feels she already has much of this world's goods. Why should she be greedy?

It is not a matter of greed! To demonstrate is to be in tune with Pure Truth and to make your life go its way toward perfection. Yes, this is why we urge you to make the demonstration. We want you to align yourself with total good and to demonstrate it. Then you will be enacting the role of partner with the great God of the Universe.

Therefore, go to work on this matter of demonstration. There is no need to compare notes with others. Remember what we told you. You are unique, and what you have to demonstrate is not what another has. If one tells you to demonstrate that he or she might see it done for himself, team up with the inner temple where the power of God meets you to advise you. The tender presences will help you to get yourself into awareness of how to handle this request. They will show you the way.

What should you demonstrate? Why, demonstrate

whatever is yours to give. The gift, when it enters through the mind of God, is always worthy, right? Then eternalize this gift without delay. Team up with the thought, whatever it is. Then push the thought into the temple where the picture can be refined, where it can be altered if needed, where it can be developed into perfection.

When all these things are completed, you will then hold the thought aloft and receive that which will team up with materiality. "What could prevent me from accomplishing my goal?" you may ask. If you continually receive the lingering thought that you don't need a demonstration, or that it is not a thing you should be doing, or that it's too grand an idea to execute or even the thought that if you demonstrate, you are "testing" God, then you will not accomplish your goal.

God is not judging your motives! God is **there for you**. Why hold back? Use what is available; cease your excuses; hold firmly to the principle involved.

Now then, we want to draw a circle. This circle is that which encompasses the whole planet earth. To be within the circle is to be within the teamwork that offers you hope that the New Age will be **Good at work**. Team up with this visualization. Hold it within your mind. Never think for one moment that the truth of what we say depends upon how you receive it! Therefore, rest assured that you are not responsible for holding the circle in place. What is within the circle is open to the Good of God, the best that is, the hope for better earth, better environment, better lives.

You, reader, will tenderly hold this image in your mind because it is your assurance of what we tell you. Eternal truth pours upon you now, truth that offers you partnership with what is about to take place—the beginning of the New Age. The picture of the circle around the earth stays firmly in place, right? Team this beautiful, reassuring picture with the best God concept you can muster. Then know that the best concept of God is your way of opening to the Greatness, the Goodness, the Majesty of the God of the Universe.

Tenderness pours out through God to all within this circle—not just the earth itself but to every living thing, be it plant, mineral or animal. Eternalize the Teammate as light that flows like pearl reflections, that which is soft, glistening, teamed up with what is purity itself. Become mesmerized with this light, but refuse any thought of awe. The Light is not an awesome thing at all. It is That Which Is because the Light must be what it is. Therefore, why stand back from what must be?

The Light which represents what God Is never turns itself this way or that. It beckons you, encourages you forward, holds you gently in its gaze. New thoughts race into your mind to turn you from a human being with doubts to a spirit entity who takes control of the teamwork. There is nothing here to give fearful thoughts, right? There is nothing here to run from.

That which teams up with you within this circle of light takes itself to and through you until you feel one with it. There is no criticism. There is only the understanding of rightness about the picture, the incoming truth, the opening of power into your life. This comes to you because you enter the eternalization that this Light is what you want, what you have always longed for, what you will never retreat from.

Be the one who evens the picture out by knowing that nothing you can do will erase the actuality of what you have held in mind. There is no possibility of your being expelled from the circle, away from the Light. This place is yours, that which is yours because the Light turns toward you with its beauty and its total smoothing over of your concerns.

That which is turned toward the Light is forever in that Light. Why resist that thought? The entering truth flows toward you that you may receive it without hesitation. Eternal truth is not hidden nor is it kept a mystery. Team up with what is yours because you in this circle of Light are one with the Source of Light.

Be into my own picture, reader. The Light that shines

within this circle shines there for me too. Those in the Brotherhood of God take their power from this Light, from this Presence, this Truth in Action. We enter into the understanding that we who are one with God never need worry about whether or not we stay in that position. That which is true with us is also true with you. We—you in the earth plane and we in this plane—become what we are because we embrace the truth that the Light never goes out.

That which is the basic element of putting Good into materiality is that Light! Now, do you understand? You— one with that Light—turn only to that Light for your resources. That Light, intent upon its mission of shining forth within the circle, reaches you with its powerful rays. The elements of that Light radiate through you to pick up what you want to demonstrate. Then it happens! The thought materializes because it has no choice.

The way to performance of the Perfect Truth or Good is to enter into this truth we give you. The way to non-production in regard to the New Age is to keep your teamwork with earth truth. There it is, the entire perspective of what is possible versus what is truly improbable. The New Age will claim your best in demonstration, but if you persist with what now exists within you from earth-mind, you will not survive nor be able to provide help and comfort for others.

We in this plane enter to get this book into the marketplace where it can be read by those who now give their thoughts to the possibilities of the New Age. We who team up with this writer in order to get the truth into the earth plane will never abandon the task. When you read this book, know we stand ready to help you with anything you do not understand or cannot accept. Be the hopeful person we eternalize as opening up to the great principles we teach, the great concept of God that we urge you to attend to. This way you will develop your understanding, and your potential will soar as that which you are reaches perfection.

The Key to Demonstration

16

What new aspect of teamwork will help my confidence in demonstrating—or manifesting—thought into substance?

Teamwork is the key to positive projection—the process that results in a thought becoming material. To make your thoughts combine with the Basic Element that produces a material result, you must understand how teamwork becomes the key.

The writer is afraid we belabor the point, but we here in this plane see how hard it is to get through the block of misunderstanding that, through the ages, has made its way deep into the human consciousness. We see people who rise to heights of greatness, but who then team up with wrong thinking and let the greatness slip away.

Why? Well, they think greatness (not fame or fortune, necessarily, but greatness in the manner of being able to accomplish what is needed and wanted) is temporary. This idea comes through earth-mind. Therefore, when they accomplish some great thing, they believe that is all they can expect for one lifetime. But it is not so.

Greatness is the expected thing when you team up with the truth from God-mind. Greatness eternalizes within those who connect with God truth and becomes the normal way of things, not a one-time thing.

We want to explain how to enter into teamwork that will create a perfect partnership with those who work along with you. This partnership is needed if you are to project thought into a material object. The way to understand the working of the law of God is to be true to that law. The way you must understand that law concerns us to the point of belaboring the method of demonstration.

It is not easy to undo the work of the ages which proclaims **you** as the sole instigator of what is accomplished in your lifetime experience. Yet, we try here in this book, step by step, repeating much of what we say initially, but yet moving ever forward to help you develop your ability to demonstrate your thoughts. Do not expect to undo the work of earth truth within the short time it takes to read this book or other books. Expect, instead, to work with the truth we present until you accept it into your very core.

The writer is thinking that what we want to teach sounds remarkably like the "miracles" of Jesus. True! Those episodes which tell about Jesus turning water to wine, of giving whatever is needed to others—whether it be food or healing—is the perfection of demonstration. Jesus became in the earth plane what you can become— one in God.

The writer is also wondering if Jesus was the only one to accomplish these demonstrations. The possibility is there for all, not just the few. Teamwork is the key, and that is our thrust in this chapter.

There are many who demonstrate the needs they see, and they find they always succeed when they enact the teamwork. But for many, the accomplishment is not understood. Therefore, they do this or that and sometimes accidentally accomplish the act. They wonder, thereafter, why it only happened once. But they tell of it as if it was a miracle. The act of demonstration is not put on any pedestal of superhuman achievement. It is not even miraculous. The demonstrated good is the product of right understanding. Therefore, we belabor and belabor the truth until we accomplish what we came here to do in these books—to show you how to be part of the teamwork, a most needed part, that produces the good in the universe upon the planet earth.

This truth is not hard, nor is it hidden from your understanding. The reason people tend to reject it, to turn away in embarrassment or to put the truth in the realm of "impossible to understand," is that they pull back from acceptance. To accept is to understand, and to understand is to demonstrate!

Be eternally tuned to God or Intelligence, or to the Hope that Brings Sustenance. God Is what God Is. No name or description is ever enough to explain what is the All in All. Therefore, you must open your mind to the fullest. Those who say "God Is this or that" have no idea what God Is. They only prattle their ignorance! Give them no attention except to smile politely. Those who prattle will try to hold your attention by denouncing the things you may want to accomplish as "devil work." You must only replay that God Is the Source of all Good. They will agree, sputter, and quote the Bible. But you know that the Bible can be misquoted for selfish purposes, so give those words no attention.

Turn to your own God-mind connection, to the Source that presents the truth to you. Enter into no debate. Enter into no public demonstration that seems to be testing "your God" as opposed to "their God." Team up with the principles we teach and work with the principles until your teamwork is what it must be to demonstrate! That which is yours to do, do! That which enters only to distract you, push away from your mind. Give no energy to annoyances. Team up with the work at hand, nothing else!

Now then, let us review the principles and recite your part in this teamwork. Begin with the principle which says that **God enters into a perfect alliance with you always, even when you do not acknowledge this partnership**. You must give more time, more thought to this principle. **God is always God**, we say to you. Therefore, you need never beg Him to enter your life, nor do you need to bargain with Him to get His help. Many of you reading this book probably have no trouble accepting this principle.

But the crux of the problem we see from here is that though many accept the principle as stated, they still do not mesh with this Greatness they call God because they have erroneous thoughts feeding into their minds. The thoughts work like poor fuel that is poured into a tank to power the engine. The motor catches, sputters, does not pull or push or whatever it is designed to do. Why? Because the fuel is incorrect! Those erroneous thoughts of yours work just in this manner.

The principle that **God Is what He Is** is absolutely necessary. You must be one with the thought that God is always there for you, to work with you, to bring you good ideas, to enlighten you, to put your lifetime experience into the thrust of teamwork that will accomplish great good. You have two principles so far. Put them where you keep your most valuable possessions. Write them down on paper. Write them across your brain. Hold them tenderly in your mind. Recite them until they are fixed and perfect. When you truly become one with these two basic principles, you will then be ready to go further.

The teamwork that we in this Brotherhood want to project to open your mind fully to your potential is now ready to be put on paper. We hope, we entreat, we pray that your attention will not wander. What is needed now is absolute attention, constant eternalizations that will become part of you so that you will no longer have to work through the principles. Then you can progress to that greatest of all feats—the demonstrations!

Being truthful with yourself is necessary at this point. What are you thinking? Where is your mind? Why are you reading this material? What do you hope to accomplish? These questions must be addressed fully, but not before other people! Address them only before the tender presences who will help you with the answers you seek. The work we do is in private, within your inner temple— not in the open marketplace. The demonstration will be in the marketplace, but not the preparation that you must do now.

Have you worked with the first two principles to the point where they are one with your spirit, your mind? When you believe you are one with them, you are ready to move forward. Entering into the next part without this first assignment completed, is to move into advanced math without the multiplication tables well in mind! Therefore, do not hurry what is basic. Work with it until you and they are one.

Eternalize, if you will, your being that is your reality. This being may look something like the human form, but not necessarily. This being that accepts its oneness with the first two principles is a teammate of God, and as a teammate grand, indeed! We do not mean to puff up your ego here—only to formulate within your thinking the way you can now think of yourself. Be assured that you who are so perfectly teamed up with God are not ordinary! God is not ordinary, and therefore, you, His teammate, are not ordinary either. This concept must penetrate your mind until the thought of being extraordinary is absolute.

There is no reason to put yourself above others! That which we say of you is true also of others. They may not know this truth, but their lack of understanding is all that separates them from you. Therefore, know that because you understand, you have taken on more responsibility than they who refuse or somehow fail to understand.

Ready to move forward? You are now one with the two principles and you accept the concept of being one with God and therefore a teammate who has great power because of your association with the One Who Is. Entertain the thought of great power, whatever it means! Do not let yourself fear power! Remember that God power is always used for the good of the universe, never that which would hurt or destroy. Become one with power.

There are some who find "power" hard to accept because they equate it with those who would rule with iron fists! The God of the Universe is not a dictator! His power is there to be used; it is not there to be forced upon any-one. Be unafraid of God power. Embrace it because it is that which will bring your good thoughts into fruition. Tenderly team up with **power** that emanates through God to your mind and out into the world. Bring your being into alignment with this **power** that will never disappoint or hurt anyone.

There is no better truth than this to solve problems, to bring forth that which is needed and desired. Team up with all that God Is, and especially team up with His **power**.

Enter now into a third principle that waits for your embrace. This principle is that **God wills your good into existence**. If you have done your homework on the first two principles and the concepts presented to you, you enter into this principle with glee. That's right—with glee! Why not acknowledge your happiness over this principle that assures you that the good that you want to project is **God's will**? Be eternally one with all that we give you. Though it seems very much step-by-step as we give it to you, it will move to work its delightful result as in one sweeping motion when you have mastered the understanding.

Yes, God's will is to produce whatever is His nature (remember the all-good principle) in the planet earth. You, His teammate, want to do this projection because it is your desire to be one who will work to move the truth forward. You have accepted the responsibility to help planet earth and her people to enter the New Age with the best results possible. The commitment is yours!

Now you know and understand what it means to be the teammate of God. We must ask you to review all this material once again as well as to review your own commitment. New truth is never easy to embroider upon our realities, for we tend to grow very, very slowly. But we speak now to those of you who have reached a point that calls for total commitment, not those who are still working to grow into the point of readiness. Those who move out into open truth will find it hard to turn away from the teamwork because they recognize the perfection possible.

Now deposit the words of this chapter into your bank where you will receive a big return on your investment. The words are the outgrowth of the work done through teamwork. They are yours. Put them into your mind and make them yours. Then invest them in your productive bank where the interest is great. You will then have the greatest of riches to draw upon, the greatest of power to focus upon the good projects that you will want to demonstrate.

Needs arise. Team up with God, His power, His truth, and work through the principles to project good answers to those needs. There! It is written in one sentence that contains the essence of our message. However, it is you who contain that which will bring the planet earth into the greatness and the goodness of the New Age because you are there to help those who want to survive and to live in this place at this greatest of times.

Evil—The Truth in Reverse

17

When I judge something or someone as evil, how is my ability to demonstrate the good of the universe affected?

The evil that we speak of here does not exist as a reality in the earth plane. Evil is only the truth in reverse—the open truth that enters your mind and is reversed instead of being accepted as it really is. This so-called evil takes up much time in the earth plane because much attention is given to it.

"That is **evil**," people pronounce of this thing or that thing, that person or this person, that act or this act. They focus their attention upon what they name evil and then hold their attention there. That is why people are sure that evil exists—because the time and attention focused upon naming it makes it seem very important.

This writer insists that there are evil things that she names as "murder, excessive greed, hurting others by not treating them with dignity and with kindness." This writer insists that we would surely name these things evil. The desire to name events, people, the many endeavors in the earth plane persists because people want to believe that there is good in the world just as they see evidence of evil.

You may think we deal only in words here and not in reality, but we assure you that we deal in the practical application of truth that will make it possible for you to use

it effectively in the earth plane. Therefore, we intend in
this chapter to offer some suggestions on how you can
team up with what is good—the God of the Universe, the
Universal Intelligence, the great Allah, the person of the
Christ as evidenced in Jesus, or whatever you want to
hold up as the essence of good.

We begin, therefore, with a denouncement of the
naming of anything, anyone, any act as evil. You scoff?
The truth is, reader, that the events and people of the
earth plane may all be under the greatness of the God of
the Universe if you will team up with this understanding.
Therefore, how can anything be named evil? The wonder
is that you do not grasp what we are getting at immediately after studying the other truths we have presented.

You want to bring good into the earth plane? Into your
life? Into the lives of those around you? Then enter into
the open truth that flows through God-mind to your
mind. That way your focus is upon that Source which
brings forth total good. We signify good by putting the
word in quotation marks. By putting it into quotation
marks and capital letters, we hope to open your mind further to what we speak of here—that "GOOD" which will
operate in the world exactly in proportion to the power
you give it. Now do you understand the point of the
chapter?

By questioning each event, each thrust of eternal truth
to the point of naming it evil, you put the power of God in
the judgment seat where it can no longer flow freely. You
effectively stop the flow of power toward the GOOD of
the universe when you rename everything evil or good.
That you can understand even better, we put the reader to
a test.

What enters your thinking when you read your newspaper? You read the stories and team up with the one
who writes them. Then you pronounce the event or the
person involved either good or evil. You denounce the
evil and think you are rising to heights of wisdom and
God-like understanding. The opposite is true. You

thwart the wisdom and the power of God when you denounce in this way.

The ones who passed this newspaper test understand what we are trying to teach here. But let us test them still further. The opening is given to you to become the teammate of the God of the Universe. That is quite in keeping with your desires, probably. The truth that enters you is that which your tender presences help you to receive. There is a constant flow. There is the marching order that teams up with you to open yourself still further to even more truth. What do you do?

Team up entirely? Or do you tell the presences that it is too much to expect you to team up with **all** that enters for you? Those of you who make excuses, no matter how humble they may sound, team up with the greater temptation that persuades you not to become all that you might become. The truth, therefore, begins to elude you. Teaming up no longer seems as important as it once did! Why?

Truth that comes to you because you enter into communication with God-mind only works when you team up with total commitment, not a sometime commitment. Energy flows through God and into you only as you open to it. But when you stand aside, perhaps thinking erroneously that it is well to keep "one foot in the world," you lose the flow of energy, you lose the stream of truth, and you even revert to earth truth for your answers.

Those who embrace God-mind truth one day and earth-mind the next day send their beings into confusion, not the certainty of accomplished good. Those who live their lives in this way do not receive an even flow of truth coupled with an even flow of energy. They receive, instead, that which releases them from their commitment!

The naming of good or the naming of evil is not to be generated within Pure Truth. That which positively reinforces the God you turn to with your full commitment is that which can turn what you in the earth plane call evil into the perfection that is the out-picturing of total GOOD. Now do you understand why you should not, out of judgment based on earth truth, name anything either good or evil?

Where is the power? Not with your eternal truth in reverse! Not with renaming whatever you see or whatever comes to your attention.

Those who enter into the perfect power of God know their Source of power. They remind themselves often that God is the Source, not man, not earth truth. They adhere to the Power That Is—the God of the Universe. No event, no condition, no person enters their gentle truth which renames them evil or even good. Why? Because there is, in reality, no evil. Therefore, why name anything evil?

Now we add yet another follow-through to this concept of evil not being reality. That which is of God is reality, that which is incorruptible, that which does not perish or pass away. This, then, is reality. That which is material in earth terms does pass away, become corrupt and does indeed open itself to disrepair. This sort of thing, then, is not worthy of being called good. Only that which is imperishable is GOOD.

The reasoning still bothers many readers even though we have made it abundantly clear! Those who write this message through the writer want to try yet again to explain the concept of our enduring good as opposed to that which some name evil.

No one who lives in the earth plane can harbor thoughts of resentment, hate, envy or other negative thoughts without paying the price according to the law of attraction which says definitely that *LIKE ATTRACTS LIKE.* Those thoughts that you hold in the dark recesses of your mind, those thoughts that you enter into but do not open to the Light which is God, redeem themselves by producing even more dark thoughts. They call you to energize them and to give them power. A lifetime experience, therefore, reflects such thoughts.

Those thoughts, however, if properly viewed within the open channel of truth—the Light which is God-mind communicating to you—will be put to rest and be turned into positive energy. That is the Pure Truth in operation. But if you deny the Light and its attendant benefits, you allow the darkness to prevail over you. Most of you understand this concept.

To understand this concept of dark thoughts turned to Light is to understand the larger concept of evil versus good. Those events that reflect the dark thoughts must be turned to the Light in order to be given a positive thrust. That is the law of thought—**that which we turn to will be our power center**. The darkness, which represents our truth in reverse, eternalizes within us as the energy of poor focus, poor understanding, poor experience. The darkness which is turned to Light, however, is opened to new energy from the tender truth of God which gently turns the dark thoughts into positive energy.

The writer wants to know if everything is basically good. The positive goodness of the Perfect Truth is in place for your use, hers and yours, reader, and the way to use it is to use it. Does that sound as if we beg the question? No! That which is GOOD is yours to use. But if you persist in giving your attention to the darkness which refused to admit the Light, then you must live your life with the truth in reverse.

The writer says that her left foot hurts when she stands and walks. For over two weeks she has been limping. Should she, she wants to know, turn to thoughts of Light or go to the doctor? This question is on the practical level we must address if truth is to be of value to you in the New Age. What about a sore foot? What about the basic needs—whatever they are?

Now we approach the crux of how to team up with the principles we bring you, how to address the exact problems. The way, dear reader, is to team up with each understanding that we present. Then use the understanding. We remind the writer, for example, that the foot she eternalizes as having severe pain is the same foot that once had no pain. The foot itself does not call to you to give it pain, does it? Then why present pain to it?

139

The left foot wants to be that which is of the positive thrust of God, right? Why, then, do you insist on presenting a picture of pain? The rule to follow here is that the principle of oneness with God means that united being of yours—the spirit and the body self, including the foot! Now the writer is thinking more sanely, more tuned to principle, to that which brings her the goodness of God. Turn to pain and you invite more pain. Turn to the wholeness of the greatness of God and you invite that wholeness. That which is good is offered you through the God of the Universe. That which offers you anything less than wholeness presents itself to you because you turn your truth on its head!

In her case, the foot presents her with a problem. What has caused the pain? What has she done to bring the pain about? That which is of God-mind addresses her on the subject. "The incoming truth on the open channel is that you have brought a strain to the entity, the foot. To turn to wholeness, you need also to be open to cause which affects that portion of your body. Team up with our best understanding here. Turn to truth, to the principles you know. Then team up with God-mind to help you to be more considerate of the portion of your body you have hurt."

As I read these words, I thought my counselor simply did not understand my problem. I had great pain in my foot, and I simply could not be the cause of it.

Enter into the quietness, writer. Enter into that which is God-mind. The operating principle here is to know that you, who are spirit, enter as spirit to the Presence which is spirit. To redeem what is physical, first redeem what is spirit. That which is physical enters itself to your care, your orders. The spirit self controls; the physical responds.

Now team up with what you know to be wholeness— that which is totally good, that which is totally of the God of the Universe. Team up with every thought that presents itself to you through God-mind, and the demonstration is complete.

The following thoughts then ran through my mind:

That which is true will remain; that which is false will drop away. The Pure Truth prevails here, and your erroneous thoughts of evil or pain will drop into the abyss of nothingness. Put your truth into the object at hand. Be assured of God's wholeness.

Sitting before the word processor, I looked down at my feet. As I did so, I became aware of something I had not noticed before. I was pushing my left foot under my chair with my right heel, and as I worked, the right foot kept a constant pressure on the top of the foot. My guidance was right—I caused my own pain. I quit hurting myself and the pain went away—totally—within three days.

The writer needs her truth if she is to put her good into the entity which is her body. Then with this truth perfectly manifested, she walks without pain. This is the way the reader, too, may team up with the principles involved in the operating truth that brings all good into manifestation.

That which manifests is good. That which promotes well-being is good. Why team up with less than good? Why turn your truth on its head? Why put the principles into reverse and order into your life that which meets no perfection standard? Why team up with what you name evil? The choice is yours, after all. Therefore, team up with every good and beatific thought that enters through God-mind! Then your life will promote the gifts of God which will enhance each entity with abundant good.

You, the One With God!

18

How is it possible for me to be one with God?

Those who read the words "one with God" and wonder what they mean, will be ready to absorb what we give to the reader in this chapter. Many think "one with God," and then they reason, "What an absurd idea!" They think oneness means they presume to be gods themselves, and they believe there is no possibility that they may put themselves into such a position.

But we say to you here and now that you are indeed gods! You enter into the full thrust of God power when you acknowledge your oneness with the Person, the Presence, the Eternal Truth in Expression, the Total Good that permeates the universe, plus all other designations given to whatever is of God. The way to absorb this understanding is to put thoughts of your inferiority into the waste can. This notion that you enter the earth plane as inferior beings is not true. That you often do not express your potential is true.

Here is the way to understand. You, the spirit who inhabits the body self, entered the earth plane to enact the growth plan made out by you with the teamwork of the great God of the Universe. You entered this earth plane with definite purpose, but the problems in expressing your plan occur when you separate yourself in thought from the One from Whom you sprang. The God of the

Universe, your All in All, your Power Base, your Goodness ready to be expressed in perfection, that which opens to Universal Tenderness, teams up with your spirit when it opens to the understanding that it is the one who entered the earth plane to be God's glory personified.

When you accept this thesis, this concept, this truth, you then step out in the wonderful power and promise of becoming what you want to be, in truth, one with God. Put away any childish thoughts of becoming the awful person who is so sin-centered that you cannot hope to kiss the very foot of God. What a terrible picture to implant within yourself.

The writer was astounded to hear, on television, that God was blamed for the earthquake in San Salvadore. "God's will," one person said. The picture of God is thus painted in its many colors according to the perceptions of those who use the paintbrush.

Various entities who teamed up with the oneness-with-God concept have led the world throughout time. Those who acknowledge the truth of these people—that they were indeed "one with God" in their lifetimes—only canonize these great examples. They do not use them as examples to follow. Why put them upon pedestals? Why place them out of reach? Why enter them into impossible thoughts? These who walked the earth and enacted their oneness with God are people as you are, reader! They did what you, too, can do, but you can do even more. Why put limits upon what can be accomplished by the entity who teams up with God?

The way to understand the truth of God is to understand who you are. The truth instated within the creation which is of God is that all energy that penetrates the earth is of God. Therefore, God enters to be part of what is made into form upon the earth. The eternalization which is you, the body self which enters to do its God work, is open to the complete good which God Is.

Those who understand what we say here race to take advantage of this knowledge! Those who do not understand clutch their truth in their fists, unable to let it perform in their environment, their entities, in their personal expression. Those who do understand hold out their arms in quiet comprehension to use their oneness with God to improve not only their own lives, but the lives of others. They enter into the work of co-creation to give back to the earth what has been consumed by the Users. Givers instate the truth once again and immediately it goes to work to bring the earth into its greatness, its energy that receives its impetus from the teamwork of God and his co-creators—those who acknowledge their oneness with the God of the Universe.

Eternalizations rise from those co-creators, eternalizations that enter the earth into its perfection. Those who put truth into the earth preserve its good by eternalizing the truth in expression. By holding to the truth that operates within the earth, they prevent erosion by those who would hold back such progress. The writer is teaming up with us here though every word is not open to her understanding. Therefore, she is a co-creator even though her understanding is imperfect. The greatness which is God demands only our acknowledged oneness, not our perfection! This idea that we must become perfect before we can work along side of the God of the Universe is the erroneous truth taught by many in the earth plane.

People who grab this "oneness principle" and try to make it work only for their own good tune in to the truth. However, they have forgotten another principle which states that **the gifts of God must be used with generosity**. The way to proliferate the powerful energy that puts your truth into expression is to use what powerful God-thought you want to put into motion not only for you but for others. Generosity expands not only to people, but to the planet as well.

The writer wants an example of what we mean. The truth that you want put into expression must not only serve you, but it must serve other people or the planet. Perfection or wholeness, for example, is not just for your body. It is for others, and it is obviously for planet earth.

145

Therefore, when you put your own bodily needs into the truth, include those of other people. Then expand even further to include the planet which gasps its breath in need of Pure Truth.

The way to perfection is not to judge yourself or others. The way to perfection is to acknowledge your oneness with God which then expands and takes over your being! That part understood, we go now to the stories of our own Brotherhood, to these spirits in this second plane of life who now work for the betterment of the truth that enters through the open channel. We, like the reader, have gone to earth many times. We, like the reader, have had many ups and downs in regard to fulfilling our growth pattern. The exact stories we told in another book, "The God-Mind Connection"* by this same writer. We told there of the deeds we did and how we grew in understanding.

Therefore, now we only want to use ourselves as examples of entities who gave themselves to the concept of being one with God and tell how that understanding changed our relationship with the great God of the Universe.

The one we tell of first is one you name the Son of God, Jesus. This one opened himself to God most fully to be the great communicator while in his last earth life. Through this communication, Jesus held to the truth he came to express until he even had to die in the crucifixion and rise from the dead. Yet many do not believe what he came to teach. This one tells the story in his own words.

WORDS FROM JESUS

The truth that opened to me while in my last lifetime made it possible for me to be the one that people thought was the perfect expression of God. That expression was why I went to earth, why I entered the body of a baby,

---

*The God-Mind Connection, 1987, first book of The Trilogy of Truth; Jean K. Foster; Uni*Sun; Kansas City.

why I grew to manhood in the land where the basic understanding of God thrived. Yet I went there with misgivings, for I had tried once before to be this perfect expression, and in that incarnation I was eternalized as the stinging enemy who controlled the gift of evil.

This seems strange indeed to the writer who expresses wonder about how I could have ever been thought of in this manner. But it happened, nevertheless. The people of that time saw my attempts to present the God expression as threats, not promises of good. They, therefore, named as "evil" what they saw me do. Though they were afraid of me, they sought to destroy me. What they were afraid of was that I brought new concepts to them about how they could be one with God.

The temerity of such a statement! "The Eternal Being thus brought to the level of man," they thought. Why could I perform such acts? "Why," they declared, "because the energy comes from the evil force that abides in this world."

Therefore, I hesitated before I came again. I observed the religious practices of that day to try to persuade people of our similarities! The truth, as always, worked its seeming "miracles," and the truth made many uneasy. This time the structure of the religion was such that they could gently put me aside. They could bring me before civil authority, not really taking the blame for what happened. They turned their truth on its head and made erroneous assumptions. Even my friends turned the truth on its head when they made me the ONE son of God.

Yet my experience in the earth plane was considered sufficient, and my truth was sustained whether or not it was understood. The New Age that comes will reveal my truth once again by showing people how to practice the truth even as I practiced it in my lifetime experience. Therefore, the way to put the life of this Son in perspective is to realize that what I did YOU CAN DO ALSO. That is my story, my truth that went into expression.

The words of Jesus completed, the chapter continued.

The energy that goes to earth from the teamwork of God to man is noticed between the planes as that eternalization of what is to be brought forth. The perfection of the good that God Is hesitates between planes, turns itself into the energy that brings earth matter into form, and then plunges into the earth plane full force. The way it works for you is that you put the thought of what is needed into the ether by way of your own eternalization.

The writer wants an explanation of what happens when one eternalizes a thought. The thought is just that—a mind action. The way to eternalize it is to act upon the thought—put it into form and shape. (We speak here of the image held in your mind as it deepens into the detailed object or substance needed.) The way to accomplish this eternalization is to put your own visualization of the needed thing into its form within your thought. If you want water, for example, then visualize what kind of water is needed—water for fish or water to drink? Put "water" into the picture as that which you want. Then you have the eternalization.

The eternalization rewards the one who activates it by teaming up with the basic truth that says that **God gives to each person whatever he is able to open himself to.** The water, or whatever, appears according to the eternalization. You may still hold to earth truth which says you must dig a well or discover a spring! But though these two things are not needed to manifest water, if you insist upon digging or discovering a spring, then the water will appear in those ways. The manner is up to you.

Be open to new ways of accomplishing things. Hold no prior limits to how substance gathers momentum to become water or food or shelter or any other needed thing. The people in the New Age will need the skills of manifestation to survive, and they must enact the energetic demonstration without bringing limits to it.

Jesus, the one who came to earth to be the one with God, put his truth into operation again and again. Yet those who knew him best later declared that Jesus must have been God Himself to accomplish what he did. They knew, they said, that they could not accomplish all that Jesus did. They did not know they too were sons of God! The energy that pours through the ether to each person who wants to put truth into motion will cause the demonstration. Therefore, use the power without hesitation, without the fear of being too teamed up with what is of the "next world," as some call the next plane.

Those who enter now to bring their stories team up with the writer to tell how it was with them when they turned completely to God power in their earth lives. This way we have examples to bring you, examples that truly worked in the earth plane, examples that may encourage you in all ways.

The first example is Teammate Thomas who produced exactly what was wanted and needed. He wanted to enact his truth in the earth plane, and his plan was to bring people new ideas about how they might travel from one place to another. They seemed to be introverted because they remained in one place most of their lives. They turned to the truth now and then, but they were becoming too ingrown, too given to practicing what they already knew instead of reaching forth for more truth.

Putting on the cloak of infancy, Thomas was born in a land that now has gone from sight. This infant was the daughter of the leader of government who allowed his children to gain much learning. Thomas chose this place, these parents, this body self and this situation so that the best in earth truth might be received. She did receive the best that was given, and she even forgot about her mission because life was full of good things.

Then one day the earth trembled, and people became afraid. The daughter of the leader became thoughtful and concerned. In meditation she teamed up with the open channel and thus began her communication with those who helped her make her God-mind connection. She knew at that point she must work out her plan while there was still time. The quake was a forewarning, you see, of the danger they were putting themselves in.

This lovely woman teamed up with God-mind to meet the needs of her people, and it was then she began to see the need of broadening their horizons. They needed contact with other peoples, other nations, other ways of thinking. Then they could better evaluate their own lives. Therefore, she began her work with transportation, and with the help of others who understood her plan, a new mode of travel was developed. This mode of travel was not without problems and a need for perfection, but she kept at the problems until they were solved.

The truth she came to demonstrate was put into motion, and people began to push beyond their immediate environment. They began to learn about other people, other ways of life. These people soon teamed up to emigrate to lands that were more solid in nature, and when the destruction of their homeland finally occurred, many were saved in this way.

The woman who entered with a plan to help people used her powerful alliance with God. Then, with help, she organized a travel plan that helped save people from inevitable destruction. Her being realized its purpose, and when she came here—to this adjoining plane—she no longer needed to return to the earth plane to enact her growth plan. However, she has entered now and then in an adult body to perform some task or other, to help people know who they are and to help them push beyond the barriers of ignorance and disbelief.

There is another one here, the entity who is called the Teammate Paul. This teammate entered life to be the wayshower who led people to active demonstrations of their truth. People were in such need of basic necessities that they were in a state of suffering and disease. Paul went to earth in the midst of all these problems to bring them what man knows as perfection of soul and body.

Because he was born in their midst, because he grew up among them, he was accepted as one brother whom they could trust. Therefore, when he burst forth with the news that it is possible to communicate to the great God of the Universe, they did not flinch or turn away. They stood their ground and looked him in the eye to study his motives, to heed his words, and to try whatever he suggested.

This entity threw caution to the wind, and with abandon he turned himself to the task of bringing people into focus on how to demonstrate truth. Most people followed him, and their lives improved. Their gardens began to grow; their stomachs were full; children thrived; people smiled with happiness. They heeded their brother and performed the seeming "miracles" that brought them into new life, new good.

The teammate himself, however, knew no rest, no peace. People besieged him night and day to perform the truth in their midst, and though he enjoined them to practice this on their own, they refused to believe that they could ever do what their brother did. Therefore, due to the crowded thought waves, the pursuance of this brother past all reason, the brother departed his body to rise in spirit to this plane. Those who had held onto him so tightly were in distress, and they believed that all was lost in their land.

And because they put their attention on the negative force—away from truth and its performance—their lands, their prosperity, their health, all began to decline. There were those who understood the brother's message, but they entered their voices too faintly and could not overcome the din of despair. Therefore, despair ultimately destroyed all that wonderful work. The teammate's truth, however, was demonstrated, his growth plan met, and therefore he is freed from having to go back again to earth to perform his growth plan.

The writer thinks that the story we have just told will discourage many of you, but do not give way to disappointment. The brother we speak of here, Teammate Paul, was not discouraged because he knew he had planted seeds among some, and though the many did not understand, the few would hold to the truth they understood and thus bring good into the world. And thus it came about that new truth entered the earth to become the perfection that God-mind always brings. To see with the eyes of spirit is to see aright; to see with the eyes of earth-mind truth is not to see what is of value.

There is still another story we want to tell you. The being who entered the planet to perform his growth plan among people who knew no god but the god of their investiture, teamed up with the body of an infant to get into the midst of these people and be accepted. Those who knew no truth except that which they brought forth from within themselves, gave their open minds to the one who grew up in their midst. They let him become their philosopher, their wayshower.

This one brother, the teammate known here as teammate Tonya, teamed up with the God-mind truth, held to it, demonstrated it around her own home, her own tribe, and thus spread the goodness that God Is. The tribesmen turned away from the bitter truth of man to the wondrously kind truth of God; they turned away from the harsh truth that emanated through the very soil of their feet to the glorious understanding of Pure Truth. They adopted peaceful ways rather than warlike ways. Their encampment was turned around, and those who ruled became those who helped their fellows in tender concern. Their leader became one who put truth into practice in practical ways.

My communicator replied to my unspoken question.

No, these are not modern stories; they show, nevertheless, the ability of one spirit to throw light upon an entire people, to bring new prosperity, new hope and new teamwork. They reveal that it is possible to promote your own growth plan and yet benefit mankind. The ones who did these things have returned again and again to do other deeds, and they update their work. They see the people and their anguish; they hear their cries for help and their wails of unhappiness. They release their own truth into the world and demonstrate it over and over.

You, too, can be one of these spirits who came to this planet at this time to help put the planet into good energy, to help people team up with God-mind truth, to demonstrate truth unlimited to help others and to teach them how to do the same. This is your opportunity, as we have had opportunities throughout the ages, to perform the Pure Truth in and on the planet earth. This truth put into expression is our Father's business, readers, it is the truth of the God of the Universe that enters now to put itself in the center of this earth.

Be assured, reader, that tender presences rise with you to perform what many will call "miracles." But though you tend to waste time wondering about all that we tell you, we hope you will quickly abandon the restraint upon your person and bring forth what must be brought forth to eternalize the needs of your planet and its people.

Gentle Presences
Speak Out

19

How can I help the new earth with new truth?

We in the Brotherhood of God have but one desire—to help you in the earth plane to express the truth that you need to express to become your potential. Therefore, we introduce the gentle presences to you, those advanced spirits who enter through the open channel, the same channel used to receive God-mind truth. As each one of these gentle ones speaks to you, you will receive explanations that will enhance your understanding of how to use the truth of God. Open your mind; open your eyes; open your heart.

Here is the first of these gentle presences.

New concepts often cause consternation among those in earth bodies. They enter into the spirit of the concept, no more. They often hold back with their reasoning powers for two reasons. First, they fear the wrath of their fellow man who may bring ridicule upon them. Second, they hold themselves aloof from the total understanding to be able to say, honestly, "I do not understand this fully, and therefore, I must wait until I do understand it before I commit myself to anything."

The human condition is such that people react with one

another before they act with the God-mind connection. This is not to be said of all people, of course. The ones who have read this book to this point certainly are ready to abandon earth ties and take the leap of teamwork that is required to be the wonderful demonstrators who will hold the New Age in their grasp. These readers want to enter the New Age with authority, under God, to perform the seeming miracles that will act upon the earth to bring forth whatever is needed.

The truth we, those called the gentle presences, bring to you is to hold you in our tender regard, our generous constraint that will team you up with the concept of **total oneness**. Be assured that those of you who are ready for the commitment of bringing forth your truth into expression will eternalize open truth to the point where it will materialize. Yes, that is what we tell you with full authority. Never hesitate to prove what we say. Move into this New Age not just studying the means, but enacting it.

Those of you who know your oneness with God now stand forth from the others. Putting your truth into the energy of the Teammate God, you put forth upon the planet what it needs. You put forth, also, the truth that will center itself within the earth to be acted upon by the planet in its re-creation process. You who stand forth to enact what we describe here will be known as co-creators with God and with all those who put their best thoughts into the powerful energy that God has to be used.

Together, we who now speak to you and those who step forth as you step forth, team up into the oneness that will prove our goals successful. We who enter to help support your commitment become the true friends you seek, the pure open tenderness that is here when you need it. Together we will hone the energy of God to a fine point that can be used readily when you need to demonstrate truth.

Now enter into our understanding of how to open yourselves to this oneness. You readers who wonder at what we tell you and those who want to be one with others in transposing powerful thought into that which is material, give us your thoughts. We are united as one— one with God-mind, one with each other, one with those who join the effort. We here, you there—it takes both groups to enter the truth into the earth. Now open your mind to us with relaxed, generous hearts.

The next gentle presence then took over the communication.

The first presence explained the "who" of our group, and I will explain the "what." Together, you and we will begin the job of putting great God truth into the earth wherever we are. There are some in the upper North American continent, others in the mid American continent, others in the southern American continent, others in Asia, Africa, Europe, the British Isles and Ireland, the teammates in Australia, New Zealand, those in the Scandinavian parts and in the various island groups. Wherever they are, these teammates who now join with us in the effort begin the work of instating the truth back into the planet.

Know that you enter into this work when you open to our oneness which will eternalize our planet into the good and gentle place we want it to be. Our work, yours and ours, is to reinstate truth into the earth and to eternalize the role of mankind in the New Age. To create this worthy endeavor,our efforts must be joined through the open channel. This channel will bring to each and every one of us the truth that is to be put into the earth and the eternalization we can hold in mind to give mankind safe passage through this difficult changeover.

The way to bring truth eternal into expression is not to individualize this truth, but to put our minds together in one effort, one generous and gentle effort. Therefore, the ones here called gentle presences team up with you there who give your commitment to this work. Together we will enter the New Age with the teamwork that will make the transition beautiful and good.

The gentle presence who will now enter will explain what you may do to put yourself on the wavelength that is our communication system.

Again there came a change of entities, and the chapter continued.

My work is involved in communication by way of the open channel. Those of you who already get your personal truth through this channel know that we can, indeed, hone our powers of teamwork by communicating through this channel. The important thing to note here is that the open channel is not just a way of communication between two spirit entities. That sort of communication is spirit to spirit—mind to mind!

Communication comes through the open channel by way of the God-mind connection that joins us in the thought that emanates from our powerful Teammate. This God-mind message comes through the channel to each of us bringing the truth that must be entered into planet earth. This truth will never lead us astray, never hurt anyone or cause us misgivings. God-mind is the generous, most tender Presence known, that which opens only to greatness and good. Therefore, to align yourself with those of us called the gentle presences is to align yourself with the God of the Universe who is the Teammate we hold as our perfect alliance with what is good and bright, centered in perfection and in wholeness.

That which holds you firm in the connection is your own mind/spirit. That which turns you to God-mind is your own being who wants oneness with your Teammate. And that which unites you with your fellow human beings and with us is that part of you who is the partner of the God of the Universe. As a team we can overcome the present circumstances that will cause the earth to turn to a new polarity. Yes, the center of all our effort is in God, the All in All, the One Who teams His Being with ours.

Then, from the Brotherhood:

Now rest a moment to review what has been written thus far in this chapter. Team up with the best understanding that you can muster at this point. Then call upon the gentle presences to help. This team of presences who now work only with planet earth, are there to help you in this work we will do together. Then, when you have rested, reviewed, teamed up with the understanding, we will move still further.

The next gentle presence who gives a message is one we brought here especially for the purpose of bringing new hope to old thoughts that need revitalizing. This gentle one shows forth the face of the Teammate, in a manner of speaking. The phrase "the face of God" is not to be taken literally, reader, but metaphorically. The face we mean is that which can be recognized by others. Now ready yourself to receive this new member of our group.

With only the slightest hesitation, the next communicator began.

The "Person of God" is what I come to speak of. The personalized God is now within the gentle presences who instate truth within the planet. Yes, the "Person" that I bring to your attention is the greatness of the God of the Universe who wants to share with you what is God's.

Now—to understand this Tenderness in Expression, this Pure God, this Eternal Truth in its Magnificence, you must open your mind to the face I speak of. The face, gentle, given to smiles, bright and happy, very open to every problem you have, teams up with you to *give*, not take. You need to "see" this face within your spirit/mind, hold this concept firmly, unshakably in your mind. Why? Because then you will want, beyond all other desires in your lifetime experience, to be the teammate who turns to this Being.

Is it clear to you? To enter into oneness with the gentle presences, you must first enter into oneness with God, and to enter into oneness with God, *YOU MUST WANT*

THIS BEING BEYOND ALL OTHER WANTS. Therefore, I present the face of God to you that you might focus on that Eminence that is your opportunity for teaming up with the best that is within the God concept. I hope you understand this presentation, for here lies the key to success in the work with planet earth and the future of earth plane living.

This writer gives a great sigh here, noting a familiarity about my speaking. This writer knew me in this last lifetime experience. Yes, she knew me as a friend who shared many spiritual insights. Yes, she is right about recognizing me, and she knows that I speak truly, as I did even in the earth plane. But now that I have ascended into higher planes, I have teamed up with higher understanding that now brings me to this work. Therefore, I make my contribution to the book in progress, to team up with the reader who wants to be part of our ongoing energy.

The total picture is now presented to you, the picture of how to be one with one another in this effort to help the planet earth and how to be one through the open channel that brings us all our God-mind truth.

Be One Who Soars!

20

Will I—will the reader—rise to the heights in manifesting eternal truth?

The eternal truth pours upon each reader—not to be looked at in amazement—but to be used in your environment. The perfect truth that is yours and yours alone is now helping you to use the eternal truth to bring wonderful good into your world. This eternalization of greatness is what we hold on your behalf that you may be certain of your potential.

That which motivates you is your own spirit self that wants to be united with the God of the Universe from which it sprang. That which holds you back from this gigantic leap forward is that human part of you that has attached itself to the earth. To bring the spirit into control, you must team up with all that is of God. Enter into the principles, the perfection, the goodness that opens to your being.

The worth of eternal truth is measured by the amount which you use. After all, what is truth unless you put it to work where you are? Therefore, understand that we press you in this matter only to get you to perform what is teamed up within you. Eternal truth wants to burst into the earth plane, burst through the entire earth situation to bring good into manifestation. Bringing forth what is good is the way to increase eternal truth that pours

161

through! When you understand this concept perfectly, you will hardly want to take time to sleep because you will want to project the marvelous good that is there to be projected!

The worth of truth is what YOU do with it! By teaming up with those who come to assist you, you will be marvelously stimulated and helped in the how's and the means of demonstration. The truth must be manifested if the earth is to make its transition without such turmoil that hardly any individual entity will be left to go forth upon the planet. We want to make it possible for the new earth to have people upon it, people who will go forth to bring goodness into the whole environment. Those who read this book must be the segment of humanity who will take this challenge to heart!

Those who team up with their potential and with our Brotherhood have every hope of teaming up with thoughts of how to survive, how to enter truth into their new situation and to know what is open to them in the way of perfection. The world is now holding its breath, holding on until we get people organized. That is why these books enter now to be studied. The entity who writes entered the adult body of one who gave it up to her in order to bring these books forth. Those entities who help her write are those who have teamed up to help the planet to become more gentle in its approach to the New Age.

We think there is no use in reviewing this book for you. The chapters speak for themselves. If you need review, you will go back over it. This chapter brings forth nothing new. It's purpose is only to rouse your teamwork that we may get the planet working in the matter of new truth and in the matter of survival of its people.

No, we will not save them all! Everyone must assess the matter and decide for himself whether he wants to survive. Those who want to survive will now take a stand for it, and they will begin immediately to march to the rhythm of the God of the Universe. They will no longer heed earth truth; they will no longer be among those who enter into negotiations for earthly power. They will, instead, turn to the God of the Universe, that open-ended concept which opens energy to their use.

Be warned, of course, that the New Age is ready to begin, but also be cheered because there is a way by which you can help reunite the truth of God with the planet's plan of created good. Give your attention to the ways you may begin right now. Grow in understanding and grow in performance. The earth was meant to be dominated by the spirit of people. But the plan went awry when people equated themselves with the physical manifestation, not the spirit which was the creative force back of every created thing upon the earth!

To turn things around, enter into the understanding of who you are in reality, not who you are in appearance. Then you will know your Source, your Teammate, your Tenderness in Expression. We seek to know your answer. Will you return to the Light? Will you team up with those who can help you with the living of your life? Will you turn to our plan to save the planet?

Energy that wants to be produced into material good hovers around you. This energy easily rushes out to people who pursue the understanding of their true identity. Team up! This is our cry to you. Team up! Be the truth in expression, be the wholeness, the perfection, the greatness that the universal energy prepares itself to be. In this way you will be what God and you want you to be—one with that which is known as God.

Enter into the role of our teammates whom we will help through the entire program of demonstration. Team up that we might help you to perform happenings known as **energy turned material**. There is really nothing miraculous involved. That this happening seems to be a miracle is only the earth viewpoint of things. You who enter into this plan will soon believe manifestation of thought by God energy is the normal, not the miraculous happening.

Those who now enter into the working out of the plan

become part of the eternal truth in operation. Put it to work, reader! Put that truth into operation in your life and in the planet itself.

This book gives its truth to you, but this will not be the last word on the subject! There will be two more books opening to this writer who will write them as she has written the others. Then you will have the total picture in hand that you may evaluate it. These books will be the textbook we told you of in the beginning. They will constitute the information that you can study, hold to your intensive thought and put into the hands of others.

Your participation in using the universal energy to express eternal truth will make the difference between a harsh and an easy turnover when the planet responds to a different polarity. The earth will turn; yes, it will shift. The winds will be harsher than you have ever seen them, but not so harsh that you cannot survive. The task at hand is for you and us to team up through the open channel that brings God truth.

Be sure of this point—that you and we are opening ourselves to a great adventure! The way may seem obscure now, but as we work together, the path will brighten. We will lead the way into the New Age where communication of this kind is most normal. We are on the verge of rediscovery, not of who we might be, but of who we really are.

This day the message of hope is given that all mankind may turn to the eternal truth of the open-ended God concept to find the way to express eternal truth in the world.

The way to truth is through the open channel, through that eternal benign way of receiving the God-mind thought. Those who have already begun this communication may already have received your instructions about the New Age. Those who now live your lives according to that growth plan you brought with you to the earth plane know that entering into the Pure Truth begins a way of life you would not trade for all the earthly powers rolled into one! Why enter into what is of earth when you can rise to heights yet unexplored? The time has come, reader, to give your being its open channel, if you have not already done so, that you may be one who soars, not one who crawls.

Put your being, your spirit/mind, into motion. Be open and receptive; turn wholly to the highest and best God concept you can muster; rise to the heights!

For more help, more encouragement, turn to the next book of the textbook series, "Masters of Greatness." It will bring you positive ways of performing the "energy plus truth projected into matter." In this book the way will be explored, but no way is certain to help you unless you try helping yourself.

Become one in mind with the God concept; become one in mind with the Pure Truth; become one who enters into the plan which will help protect planet earth and envelop her in truth.

Witnesses From the Next Plane Offer Their Own Observations on Saving the Earth

Those who write with me, advanced spirits in the next plane who are of the Brotherhood of God, interrupted our regular work one day to say that a legion of witnesses from their nearby plane was ready to speak to me. They wanted to give their testimony in regard to helping planet earth center itself in truth.

The Brotherhood said, "Many who wish to give testimonies come because they love the planet and want consummate good for it. Others enter to urge you and the readers to help with this project we call Earth-Saving. They believe that what they and you can do together is too important to be ignored."

In the section that follows, six witnesses are included as representative of the many messages I received. Those who witnessed to the coming New Age did not trade on the names and reputations of their last earth lives; they preferred anonymity. Their only concern was to tell others that the world is in jeopardy and to insist we begin now to reinstate truth.

FROM A FARMER

One of my first communications came from a college educated man who was both teacher and farmer. His greatest love had been working his farm.

In my last lifetime that which interested me most was

the earth itself, its productivity, its use in bringing forth riches.

Put better truth into the earth and it produces better growth, better energy, better crops, better animals. The earth must be replenished, and fertilizer will not do the trick. Fertilizers like I used only touched the surface and temporarily caused the soil to produce well.

What has happened is this. Perfection, which is the earth potential, has eternalized within the earth's core. It is here the generating power center unites with every cell of every particle that creates whatever earth is. That means that from the center of the earth pure substance enters into the basic energy of all that is.

Therefore, this planet must be thought of from the inside out, not the outside in. The weighing of the eternal worth of this truth substance is eventually realized when you know that without it, the earth collapses. This work of renewal interests me here, and I work with it each and every moment.

That which is my reality now opens completely to project Earth-saving. Team up with those who witness, for they give you this great opportunity to be part of the re-creation of the earth. That is my witness.

PROJECT EARTH-SAVING

The next witness to speak indicated a sense of urgency.

The person that I was in the earth plane came here full of excitement over teaming up with whatever I might find. Ideas that came with me went to the guide who met me, and this one tenderly led me to greater heights of expression. The entire openness here teams up with each spirit who has an open mind, and this spirit then soars with potential. The person that I was (in the earth plane) never talked much of replenishment of the earth. But when I came here, I could see and I could hear the pain of the earth itself! This pain is evident when we, who now see with new insight and true understanding, team up with the way earth really is.

I give my witness here that those in this plane who enter into Project Earth-Saving team up with what must be done RIGHT NOW. There is no time to consider the matter; that time is long past. There is no time to resist what is printed on these pages, for the time grows near when the matter must be resolved one way or another. Therefore, put your best effort into the project. By teaming up, we will at least rescue earth from destruction. Perhaps we can even get the new truth installed in order to make the upheaval less traumatic for those who will continue to live in the earth plane.

You will surely join in this effort, won't you? Surely you want to help this planet to survive and to heal and to recreate and to get new truth instated in its core! Those who greet you from this plane enter their strong opinions so that you may be moved to something besides intellectual consideration of the problem at hand—the renewal of the earth!

When I lived on earth, I had a wonderful life. The experience was meaningful and has helped me immeasurably to grow in spirit. That is the purpose of the lifetimes. The reason we enter the earth plane is to team up with bodies and express our truth. Therefore, we do not want to lose this precious planet, for creating another to take its place is a long, long process.

The writer wants me to say my name. She wants me to give some idea of who I am. She thinks my name might help in some way. The one that I was gives you my witness, and that is my gift. The name? Well, it was (a symbolic name) who entered his truth the best he knew.

HELP FOR THE POOR AND THE HUNGRY

The spirit/mind who offers the following witness, I was told, spent her last lifetime working with the poor and the hungry. In this witness, she not only expresses her concern over the earth itself, but also about those who have needs greater than earth-mind can meet.

I want to renew my work within the planet by giving

my observations to those who want to help the planet. At the same time I want to help those who live upon its face. Those who are concerned about the poor of earth may agree with my thinking more rapidly than those who consider only the planet.

Those whom you see as poor, wretched, not able to care for themselves for whatever reasons, need eternalizations that eternal truth can strengthen. The poor need strong eternalizations that will put a prospering influence within their beings, not within the temples (churches) which try to help these poor ones through overt means. Those you know to have physical needs believe that their needs may be met only from the physical aspects of earth. The way, however, to meet these terrible needs is through the eternalization process.

The eternalization process opens people to their real need—hunger for partnership with God. It does this by entering a picture of perfection within their thoughts. In turn, their thoughts eternalize their need to be one with God into the ether where the physical meets the thought. Thus the need is met by manifestation. In this way people's needs may be met by the millions, not by the hundreds!

What can you do to alleviate hunger except to feed a hungry family, perhaps? What can you do to solve the problems of those who are destitute? The task seems horrendous, does it not? The task teams up with what is thought impossible, right? Then why team up with this method at all? The way to solve problems like these terrible ones that cause real physical suffering is to get to the truth of the matter.

That truth rests within the teamwork of the great Goodness of the Universe, that which enters to team up with needs in order to manifest solutions. That is the obvious answer! Why, then, do people who live on earth enter their teamwork into that which has never worked before? Why not open their minds to new avenues of solution? Why not open the mind to the teamwork that really works?

CREATING A PLAN FOR EARTH

This witness describes a hopeful, optimistic and logical plan that will involve readers who want to participate in the re-creation of the earth. By way of background, this spirit/mind likens the earth plan to an individual growth plan. Just as a spirit entity makes a plan which he or she intends to follow in a forthcoming life experience, so does the earth itself require such a plan before the New Age.

New ways to project the earth's plan have been developed in this plane. Those who work with the re-creation of the planet are the leaders in using the law which states that **the earth must repond to the mind.** That is eternal law. Therefore, what is in the mind of earth, what is in its thinking part, must be considered important enough to devote great time to it.

The growth plan of earth. What wonderful opportunity lies in its formulation! The energy that emanates from Universal Intelligence energizes the plan. But yes, we must first have a plan. Those in this plane have formulated a beautiful plan for the fruitful earth, but you there in the earth plane must add the refinements. You who team up in this work can give us your ideas about how the earth must be when the New Age comes.

Those who reach out with their minds and stretch with their teamwork to be part of this process will see the opportunity they have to provide good to those who live on earth. When the powerful teamwork (between earth and the open truth) pulls the earth from its present axis, the upheaval will be great. However, if there is planning on your part, there will be places on earth where people may go to live through the changeover, through the period of putting new truth into action.

Those of you who want to help with the plans must be open to working with us. Therefore, call upon your helpers, the tender presences, who stand by. Team up with them to enter into this work. First, put more truth into yourself. Second, operate your skills in communication that you may team up with us and with the Great Intelligence. That is the plan that we want to perform here—the teaming up of those in this plane with those of you in earth plane who want to help in this endeavor.

FROM A WORKER IN THE FIELD

The following witness explained how he came to get involved in the work of restoring God truth to planet earth.

The truth that came to me here suggested that I had neglected to give anything of value to the earth. That which had held me in its lap, I took for granted. But earth gave its good to me nevertheless. The truth tells me that even though I am not on the earth plane, I can do much in the way of inserting truth back into the planet where I lived many, many lifetimes.

Therefore, my life now is devoted to this work, and each time I help one of the advanced spirits, I myself grow in nature. The way I was when I last lived on earth is not the way I am now. The way I see things now is through the eyes of one who is open to the Universal Intelligence, the Great Energy that is the eternalization of everything that is good and pure, templed with the beautiful.

Because I am a worker in the field of earth-saving, I grow in understanding and I grow in spirit. I tell you this to help you understand that it is possible to wrest the imperfect part from your being and to insert the good even as we work with earth to do this same thing. We—you, I, the planet itself—team up to bring God's own purity into the eventual perfection of both earth and spirit.

EARTH-SAVING CONTRACT

The person I was in my last lifetime matters very little now. I am not that person now because I am one who has lived through many lifetimes, not just the last one. My name was known among those who wanted peace, who wanted to be free, who wanted to end war.

With this curt, matter of fact opening, this witness got right to the point of his message.

Those who want to help their planet get rid of impurities, those who want to put perfection into the very core of the plant, may now read and agree to the following:

CONTRACT

Better truth is needed by planet earth. The entity that I am, the reality of my being which is spirit/mind, notes the need. The truth opens itself to me now, and I agree to help with the project called Earth-Saving.

Signature _____

As you mentally sign the contract, truth pours through, and you team up with those in this plane who devote themselves to Project Earth-Saving.

We here in this plane urge you to join us in truth work that will save the planet we care about.

Review of Principles In "New Earth—New Truth"

The spiritual law that WE ARE INDEED ONE WITH GOD must be understood and put to work if we are to improve our lives, help the planet to survive and to bring our truth into manifestation. That WE ARE ONE WITH GOD is what this book, "NEW EARTH—NEW TRUTH" is all about. To repeat this statement AND to understand it perfectly is to be that oneness in expression.

However, because the concept undoes a large body of religious beliefs, because it encompasses such vast energy and such vast promises of accomplishment, this book explains many principles that are, in and of themselves, the bits and pieces of the whole understanding, the WHOLE LAW.

Here are the principles taught in "New Earth—New Truth:"

THE GOD-MIND PRINCIPLE

People have the resources to create a perfect planet and perfect lives because perfection is possible through their teamwork with the God of the Universe. Teamwork begins with the individual open mind that enters into communication with those who enact the Holy Spirit. Then it develops into a partnership with God. This perfect partnership brings each teamed up truth into the earth experience because manifestation is the law by which God operates.

The Holy Spirit—or Brotherhood of God—is made up of advanced spirits who are the counselor, the comforter and the teacher. To make this communication work, each person must make a conscious acceptance of the Brotherhood. With this communication in operation, each person is led into an individual God-mind connection—the individual mind tuning in to the flow of wisdom that God has for each person.

The partnership that you will use will then enable you to have the wisdom needed to open all mysteries, to bring forth that which is required for sustenance, or to produce that which will be put to good use in the earth. The partnership is the basis of your new understanding which will never depleat, which will never grow tired or weak, which will not only maintain life but will prosper it.

THE PURITY PRINCIPLE

Because God only creates Good, nothing that is impure can withstand the truth which proclaims purity to all. Therefore, no planet can survive in the universe with the pollution earth now accumulates. To attain purity, the earth must receive new ingestion of truth. People, when they understand that they can affect this unity of truth and earth, may begin immediately to reinstate within the planet what others have depleted.

Purity is one of God's gifts—a gift that people can accept with the help of the Brotherhood. Purity enters as that irresistable energy that commands the material elements to give up impurity and reinstate whatever is needed to become purity in expression.

THE PRINCIPLE OF GOD

When God is spoken of as principle, we understand that God—or all that is Good—pours out opportunities to those who live on planet earth. God principle rises above the threadbare earth truth but never forces itself upon anyone. The principle stands inviolate, incorruptible, open to the use of mankind.

To make use of this principle, hold the mind/spirit

open to the Mind of God, to that principle of Good. Then, whatsoever is pure, whatsoever is good, whatsoever is of gentleness will proclaim itself in your entire experience. Because God is only capable of producing good, it is impossible to use the Teammate to enhance your image and to gain power over others.

THE PRINCIPLE OF SPIRITUAL GROWTH

When people open their minds to new understanding, they grow in spirit. Old concepts, old beliefs hamper the growing spirit. To raise the individual spirit into the Mind of God, one must increase personal understanding by opening the mind to new concepts, new principles. The person who opens his mind to new growth will allow the God-mind connection to form. That connection then opens the individual to more and greater understanding, and in that way, the spirit grows and grows in unlimited ways.

THE PRINCIPLE OF RECEIVING GOD'S GIFTS

Tender or gentle presences are known as God's graduate students, those who hover in the earth plane to help people express their God truth and thus become their potential. These presences enter the earth plane as the outreach of the Brotherhood, that body of helpers who enact the Holy Spirit of God.

If people cannot acknowledge these spiritual helpers as real, they cannot open their minds to the gifts these tender presences bring. To accept the reality, or spirit as real, people must acknowledge the helpers—those who operate as the generous outworking of God.

THE PRINCIPLE OF DEMONSTRATION (MANIFESTATION)

The prime mover of truth into material form is the individual, not the God of the Universe, not the Brotherhood.

Each person unifies a demonstration by noting any urgent need or desire and by working with the tender presences who help to refine the visualization and put it into the perspective of God truth. Finally, the prime mover acknowledges the ultimate power of the God of the Universe Whose energy proves the truth by producing it as the desired condition or by bringing it into earth material.

THE PRINCIPLE OF THE TURNABOUT

The person you are must give way to the person you can be with the teamwork of the tender presences and teamwork with the God of the Universe. You can be whatever truth gives to you. Therefore, you can be the authority that actualizes the God message. Yes, you have the potential of being whatever it is that God IS! To open your mind to this understanding, you must embrace the principle of the turnabout, the one who turns toward the Perfection which is God, the Optimum Energy which is God, the entire partnership with all that God IS.

THE TEAMMATE PRINCIPLE

This principle widens and broadens the God concept. The Brotherhood reveals the greatness of the Kingdom (that Bright Energy that focuses on Good) to each individual who enters into the relationship of working with the Teammate, God. The Teammate is not a venial Servant, no! This Teammate wraps the tenderness of God around your being, wraps the purity of God around your waning energy, twines the pearls of wisdom into the fabric of that which you truly are. This Teammate enters into no agreement or contract with you! That which God IS opens to anyone who teams up with what God IS. Therefore, recognize the Teammate Who works with your being to bring greatness into the earth plane in the form of righteousness, in the form of goodness, in the form of purity manifested in the earth and in the body self. Whatsoever is good is the province of the Teammate. Whatever and whoever want what the nature of God IS may have that allness.

THE PRINCIPLE OF UNLIMITED GENEROSITY

Taking God's gifts and using them renews the Source; it does not deplete it. The "teteract truth"—that which comes from earth-mind—insists that there is only a limited amount of anything. But "peterstet truth"—God-mind wisdom—pours out in unlimited quantity whatever the individual is able to receive. God gives what is His to give because it is His nature to give. There is no self interest; there is no threat implied.

THE PRINCIPLE OF
EARTH ENERGY IN ACTION

Whatever proves itself in earth-mind must eventually betray what is for the total good. The earth truth that man has established focuses on the good that man becomes when he uses the forms and the established methods of the social environment. But when this good manifests, it either betrays others or else it betrays the one who operates by the principle.

The earth truth focuses on poverty, on depleted resources, on the wickedness of mankind, on the outrageous assumption that only man enters opinions that matter in the establishment of the planet. Then, by establishing laws, by pressuring entities to open to their way of thinking or by establishing private movements, earth truth tries to produce what is good.

This understanding creates weakness which is not established in the law of the planet. The earth responds only to that creative impulse which is God. The planet did not push itself into being because man insisted that it must do so! The planet contains that spiritual quality which is behind all created endeavors. It is not merely material in nature—without inner goodness, without the

179

spark of gentle growth and development that enters into each living thing.

Therefore, earth truth (which man has wrought from poor observation of what is real and what is not) goes out in its weakness and establishes what is weak. But, the truth of God moves in the environment of earth with the authority of pure understanding of what will team up with true good, true energy, the true way to get perfect answers, perfect understanding.

THE PRINCIPLE OF WHAT GOD IS

To perfectly understand this principle, each individual must understand what God IS. That concept is never perfect, but it can be enlarged, it can be open to your consciousness which will grow in insight. The God of the Universe holds no perfect description of what God IS. Even those who enter the higher planes of reality do not present a description that will give perfect understanding. Therefore, realize that to define God is to limit God!

The Pure Truth that enters each individual who teams up with the Teammate, the Partner, will be that guide as to what God IS. Therefore, do not even try to put God into words or into pictured form, but hold this concept open.

That which is God, that which emanates through what God IS, brings the true perfection into planet earth, into the total universe, and into your own lifetime experience. What could hold more promise? What could be more worthwhile? **Therefore, to hold the principle of God in your being is to know that you have that oneness with what God IS**.

THE ALL-GOOD PRINCIPLE

To perfect your own understanding of the nature of what is God, undertake the thought behind the "All-good Principle." This thought expresses God as that unequivocable good that pervades the universal energy.

That GOOD undertakes its mission—to express in this universe as the positive creative force that provides tenderness, gentleness, benign thought, and creative energy that pours into and throughout what IS.

To further your understanding of the nature of God, divorce yourself from the idea that there is an opposite force, a force that beleaguers mankind, that touts evil understanding or that pursues the gentle truth in order to destroy it. No, you cannot give blame to the evil forces in the universe. You must assume the burden, if it is a burden, to cement into your consciousness that All-good Principle. Then, you will realize that to put this All-good Principle to work in your own environment, all you need do is to accept it and work with it. Herein lies the core of understanding that mankind must accept if he is to function as one with that perfect Goodness that we name the God of the Universe.

THE PRINCIPLE OF GOD'S ALLIANCE WITH EACH INDIVIDUAL

God is the Partner who will bring personal and eternal truth into manifestation—whether a person acknowledges that partnership or not. This principle works without the need of each individual begging or bargaining with God. It works even though the individual does not perfectly understand how the partnership works.

But what closes the door of an effective partnership are the thoughts of earth truth that crowd out the partnership, that enter their own fragile energy that interrupts the flow of wisdom and the energy of accomplishment.

THE GOD IS ALWAYS GOD PRINCIPLE

To know that God is always there for you—to work with you, to bring you good ideas, to enlighten you, to put your lifetime experience into great joyous endeavors—is to understand what you must know if you are to demonstrate or manifest your truth. Work with this principle until it is indelibly written within you, until it becomes that which you are!

THE GOD WILLS YOUR GOOD INTO EXISTENCE PRINCIPLE

When you bring this principle into your mind, you no longer doubt the greatness of God! The will of God—that which is sought after—is that which you want to manifest in your life! How can this be true? Because God IS the Teammate, the Partner Who wants your highest good. That good is not opened to you in terms of unhappy events or in ways that bring you personal unhappiness! The will of God is that GOOD that is your best, your highest expression of God.

Use this principle to understand that when your truth pours out to you, this is the energy that teams up within you. When this truth takes form, it is your truth manifesting. When this same truth manifests into changed conditions or into performing seeming miracles, this is the God of the Universe Who empowers His Will to your lifetime expression.

THE PRINCIPLE OF THOUGHT

That which we turn to is our power center. To use the power which is the God of the Universe, turn only to that which God IS. To make use of the powerful thrust of good which can transform ANY situation, any entering thought into universal good, turn only to that Source of Good. To call what you see "evil" or to call it by other similar names is to thwart the power of the God of the Universe! That which you name "evil" becomes your power center, not that which is God. The perfection, the powerful thrust of energy that you and your Teammate bring into the earth plane must be recognized, must be held tightly within your being. Otherwise, you hold only vague promises of the loving God Who wants you to have that which is good.

People become confused. They ask, "Is God a powerful Entity or not? If God IS that which is powerful, why do good people have problems?"

The misconception is that God IS the powerful Being Who controls the center of your being. Not so. God gives you free will; God does not control you. Only you control you! Therefore, when you team up with the God of the Universe you bring total commitment to the principle we state here. This principle works in your life because it must work there.

THE PRINCIPLE OF ETERNALIZATION

This understanding results from the teamwork between God and man. That thought which is activated by man, purified by God, then brought into the earth plane in material form is what is called eternalization. To use this principle, mankind must open to the understanding that God IS the ultimate power, the creative substance, the true energy that operates as reality. That powerful concept is yours to use as the teammate of the God of the Universe.

GLOSSARY

advanced souls—All souls (spirit entities) come to planet earth with growth plans. Those who enact these plans in their earth lives are referred to as "advanced."

agape love—There are many kinds of love. Agape refers to love that helps one another, not a love that encompasses a person with affection.

automatic writing—This kind of writing is a process the writer uses to record the mind to mind communication between her and the Brotherhood of God. It ties into the writer's inner perception of thoughts that pour into her open mind through the open channel.

Bible—A collection of stories, history and remembrances that gives the progression of thought about God. It is a guide for living, divinely inspired, but it is not the only word of God. The word of God comes to each individual as a flow of wisdom, and the Bible—at best—is but one source of wisdom. God—a living, pulsating, vibrant energy—is the Source of Pure Truth, not a Bible—any Bible.

Brotherhood of God—Advanced spirits stay nearby in the next plane of life to enact the work of the Holy Spirit. They are the counselor, the comforter, the teacher who work with those in the earth plane who open their minds to them. These spirits are helpers who want to help people team up with the God of the Universe to receive eternal and personal truth.

channel—An individual who is called a channel is only proving that there is communication possible between those in the earth plane and those in the next plane of life. Anyone can be a channel through which the Mind of God pours individual and eternal truth.

channelled writing—When mind to mind communication is written, it is often called channelled writing. However, all inspired writing—be it poetry, stories, essays, even music or artistic expression is to be considered channelled.

christ—This is a concept of oneness with God. Each person can consider himself or herself the Christ in the sense of that oneness. When we acknowledge the Christ, we acknowledge our oneness with God.

devil—Here is a concept many people hold in mind to explain what they call "evil." This concept of an evil presence within a person diminishes the concept of God by keeping the individual focused on the absence of what God IS.

demonstration—Basically, demonstration is the process of producing your thought into the physical world. The success of the process is predicated upon a person's understanding and application of spiritual principles.

earth-bound spirits—When souls — or spirits — separate from their bodies and live in the next plane of life, some cannot let go of their earth life identities. These spirits are called "earth-bound."

earth-mind—Earth-mind goes no further than man has gone. It proves its beliefs in material substance, historical data, scientific observations. Earth-mind also embraces religion as a worthy effort to reach God. But God is often demoted to that which holds society together in values, not a personal entity Whose vastness is yet to be proved in individual lives.

energy—Enate power that rises from your truth—either God-mind or earth-mind.

entity—When an individual is called an "entity," the reference is to the inner being or spirit self.

emptying (yourself)—This is a process of clearing the mind of tempermental thoughts and personal ego in order to receive God's truth. Meditation, willingness to let go of personal beliefs, and trusting your highest concept of God are examples of emptying.

eternalization—This term refers to the goal or object you visualize along with the helpers from the Brotherhood. They and you work with your God truth to visualize what is needed, what is wanted. Then, the three in one—the Holy Spirit, the spirit of the individual and the power of the God of the Universe produce any generous and worthy thought into earth substance.

gentle or tender presences—These spirits work within the Brotherhood/Holy Spirit to reunite your being with God spirit. With the help of these presences, those in the earth plane can meet every need or concern with positive, perfect understanding. With their help, each person can be useful in his society and can help meet the needs of others as well as himself.

God-force—This term refers to the power of God that acts according to truth principles. This power manifests thoughts into things.

God the Father, God the Judgment, etc.—Terms which indicate the extent of the concept people have about God. Words that follow "God" indicate what it is that people believe.

God of the Universe—This designation is meant to open your concept of God to the furthest reaches of your mind. The God concept must be expanded if it is to meet your best expectations. The smaller the God concept, the smaller the expectations; therefore, the Brotherhood tries to help each individual to open his/her mind to all that God Is.

God-mind—The unrestricted and unlimited Mind that produces a flow of wisdom that anyone can tap into is called *God-mind*. This truth that flows with a steady impulse wants to connect with the individual mind/spirits who reach out to become one with the God of the Universe. In this text the God-mind truth is called "peterstet"—that which satisfies perfectly, that which never runs out of energy.

God-mind truth—See *God-mind*.

God-self—The entity or person who is teamed up with God.

God's emissary—A person who lives the truth of God.

growth—When a person accepts truth and lives it, spiritual growth occurs. This growth is that which becomes a permanent part of the spirit self.

growth plan—Before a soul or spirit enters an infant body within the womb, that entity made a plan to achieve oneness with God. This plan, if it was true to the nature of what is God, was a cooperative venture between the God of the Universe and the individual.

Holy Spirit—The Counselor, Comforter, Teacher which is the activity of the Holy Spirit is centered in those advanced spirits called the Brotherhood of God.

inner self—The reality of each person is the inner self or spirit/soul. This inner self has lived many lifetimes and will never die.

inner temple—To help us in our spiritual growth, it is recommended by the Brotherhood that we create within us an inner temple. This temple is a meeting place for us and the Brotherhood. It is here that we study, meditate, learn.

Jesus—The Brother of Brothers (Jesus) became the outward manifestation of the inner being who lived his life according to his growth plan. Jesus the man reflected his inner self who enacted his oneness with God.

love—This term cannot be understood in human terms, for experience gives us erroneous ideas about love. Tenderness is the ultimate spiritual expression of total support and caring. Love is a servant of tenderness and bows before the ultimate expression because "love" gives and receives. Tenderness only gives.

manifestation—See *demonstration*.

mind/spirit—The mind is separate from the brain. The brain is physical—material; the mind is spiritual. When the term "mind/spirit" is used, it refers to the reality within us—the soul or spirit which is capable, under any and all conditions, of connecting to all that God Is.

New Age—The time now appears on the horizon when the earth must reinstate purity into its being. When this time comes, nothing will be as it was. Those who heed the truth of God, however, will help both planet and mankind to survive, to flourish and to live in total teamwork.

next plane of life—The earth plane is where our spirit selves—our souls—express in human form. The next plane of life interpenetrates the earth plane, and it is here that the Brotherhood of God work as the outreach of the

Holy Spirit. It is also a place of coming and going—spirits leaving the earth plane and spirits preparing to re-enter life on planet earth.

open channel—The means by which the Brotherhood of God works with each individual to help bring about the God-mind connection.

partnership—When we accept truth from God and decide to live only that truth, we are in partnership with the God of the Universe. When we accept the Brotherhood of God as our Counselor, Comforter and Teacher, we are in partnership with the Holy Spirit.

peterstet truth—Personal and eternal truth from the Mind of God to the individual mind is called "peterstet" because it satisfies and enlightens each mind/spirit who receives it and uses it.

pontification—That which is thought, spoken or written in regard to spiritual matters.

prayer—Religionists practice prayer to bring mankind into mental attunement to their God concepts. Prayer offers hope, consideration and an opportunity for reverance. Prayer is seldom thought of as communication between God and man. It is usually a ritual connecting man to a God he cannot hope to understand.

reincarnation—Living one lifetime after another as men and women, as various nationalities, as members of all races, we have an opportunity to enact our growth plan and enact our oneness with God. Reincarnation is God's plan which gives people many opportunities for spiritual growth.

religion—An organization which brings people together in churches for the purpose of worship and to turn them into good workers. Generally, religion keeps people from their individual discovery of God.

replenishment—When people draw upon the gifts of God, when they respond to God truth, they replenish the earth and their lives with what is the nature of God.

Satan—Satan and the devil are not the same. Satan is the Old Testament personality who gives the personification of evil in many fictional stories. But Satan did not tempt people. He was the questioner who asked questions that people needed to answer and to understand their relationship with God.

spiritual law—Any God truth that operates within the universe as law—as that which must come about.

soul—See *inner self*.

teamwork—This term is the basic strength of the work of spirit, for without the teamwork of the Brotherhood/Holy Spirit and the God of the Universe, there can be no accomplishment of permanent value. Teamwork takes each one who understands its strength into the realm of the masters who can bring earth materiality from the seed of God truth. *Team up* is the directive to join with the God of the Universe and the Brotherhood of God.

templing—By bringing God truth together with the inner spirit, the two are templed, or perfectly joined.

tenderness—See *love*.

tension—Tension, tone and vibration are interconnected. Each person determines his spiritual tension or outreach for what is God; tension determines the spiritual tone which, in turn, affects the vibration of the spirit which probes for the flow of wisdom from God-mind.

teteract truth—This earth-mind truth encourages mankind toward his potential, but then this truth lets people down, for it does not have an extended, far-reaching and ultimate goodness within it.

thought-form—The human body is a thought-form, for it is the manifestation of that creative goodness which emanates through God. Other thought-forms are the manifested thoughts that we, with the help of the God of the Universe, bring into being.

tome—One book of a series of books which contain the truth that God has to impart.

tone—See *tension*.

truth—Anything you believe in is your own truth. Truth, as you take it within and work with it, develops the fabric of your lifetime experience. Your truth consists of powerful thoughts that become the center or focus of your mind/spirit.

vibrations—See *tension*.

wetness—When the Brotherhood of God uses the word "wetness" or "wet," the words denote discouragement in its various forms. "Wet truth" is earth-mind truth that leaves an individual without hope. "Wetness" is the quality of inferior truth that never comes from the Mind of God.

Also by Jean K. Foster:

The God-Mind Connection
An account of the writer's communication with spirit counselors called The Brotherhood, this book provides instructions on finding and making your own personal God-mind connection. The first volume of a powerful trilogy, Jean Foster's book offers clear information on how to discover your true purpose and destiny.

141 pages, perfect bound, $8.95

The Truth that Goes Unclaimed
In this second book in the *Trilogy of Truth*, after "The God-Mind Connection," Foster explores in detail the specific steps the reader may take to establish his personal God-mind connection and allow it to be a powerful force in his own life: how to clarify goals, form a greater God-image, build an Inner Temple, and experience truth in practical ways.

174 pages, perfect bound, $8.95

Eternal Gold
In a trilogy that helps readers claim the perfect truth available to each of them in everyday life, this final book reaches forward into powerful new concepts and methods for enhancing life in every re-

spect. Here the reader is shown how to deal directly with God and thus to address problems of health and prosperity as well as individual issues. Eternal gold is the God truth each one may claim, making life truly richer and more blessed.

143 pages, perfect bound, $8.95

Epilogue

What happens to us when we die? Where do we go? Will God punish us for our wrongdoing? Will we see Jesus? What will life be like in heaven? Will I join my parents or my spouse?

All of these questions and many more are answered in the fascinating stories told by departed spirits of what happens when we die and leave the earth plane.

According to the spirit entities contacted by the writer, the next plane of life is similar to the earth plane with some major exceptions. The greatest surprise, they say, is that "here everyone communicates by thought. They create by thought, and they even get what they need and desire by way of thought. If you want a stand of redwood trees in your backyard, that's what you get."

173 pages, perfect bound, $9.95

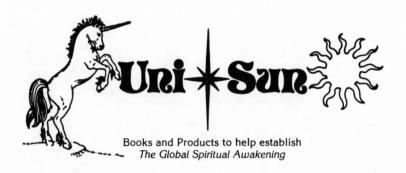

Books and Products to help establish
The Global Spiritual Awakening

Jean Foster is an important new writer, a very clear channel and one of the many now appearing to show the way to the New Age. Jean Foster's first three books, *The Trilogy of Truth*, have presented an introductory exposition of spiritual principles and have earned her an enthusiastic following.

"New Earth—New Truth" is the first book of her latest trilogy. It will be followed soon by "Masters of Greatness" and "Eternal Teamwork."

We at Uni*Sun will continue to do our best to publish books and offer products that make a real contribution to the global spiritual awakening that has already begun on this planet. For a free copy of our catalog, please write to:

Uni*Sun
P.O. Box 25421
Kansas City, Missouri 64119
U.S.A.